# The First Year Matters: Being Mentored . . . in Action!

## This book belongs to

New teacher's name _____

School _____ Grade level _____

Phone _____ Email _____

## My mentor's name is _____

School building _____ Room no. _____

Phone _____

Email _____

## New-teacher support group contact information

Name _____ Phone _____ Email _____

Name _____ Phone _____ Email _____

Name _____ Phone _____ Email _____

Date I received this book _____ Date I completed this book _____

# About the Author

**Carol Pelletier Radford** is the Program Director for a *Transition to Teaching* federal grant, which is located in the Center for University, School and Community Partnerships at the University of Massachusetts Dartmouth. She received her Ed.D. from Harvard University in 1996 where she focused her studies on teacher professional development and the role of the cooperating teacher in preparing pre-service teachers. In more than twenty years as a public school teacher, she has received numerous teacher leadership awards, among them the prestigious Christa McAuliffe Fellowship sponsored by the U.S. Department of Education. She is the author of four books: *Techniques and Strategies for Coaching Student Teachers, Strategies for Successful Student Teaching, Touch the Future: TEACH!,* and *Mentoring in Action: A Month-by-Month Curriculum for Mentors and Their New Teachers.* For the past thirteen years, she has worked as the Director of Practicum Experiences and Teacher Induction at Boston College. In her current position at the University of Massachusetts, she teaches graduate courses for district mentors and is actively engaged in preparing prospective math and science teachers for New Bedford and Fall River schools.

# The First Year Matters

# Being Mentored . . . In Action!

## A Month-by-Month Reflective Guide for New Teachers and Their Mentors

### Carol Pelletier Radford

University of Massachusetts Dartmouth
Center for University, School and Community Partnerships

Upper Saddle River, New Jersey
Columbus, Ohio

**Library of Congress Cataloging-in-Publication Data**

Radford, Carol Pelletier.
   The first year matters : being mentored—in action! : a month-by-month reflective guide for new teachers and their mentors / Carol Pelletier Radford.
     p. cm.
  Includes bibliographical references.
   ISBN-13: 978-0-205-58555-7 (alk. paper)
   ISBN-10: 0-205-58555-8 (alk. paper)
   1. Mentoring in education—Handbooks, manuals, etc.   2. First year teachers—Supervision of—Handbooks, manuals, etc.   I. Title.
   LB1731.4.R33 2009
   371.102—dc22
                                                     2008018110

**Executive Editor and Publisher:** Stephen D. Dragin
**Editorial Assistant:** Anne Whittaker
**Marketing Manager:** Krista Clark
**Production Editor:** Gregory Erb
**Editorial Production Service:** DB Publishing Services, Inc.
**Interior Designer:** Denise Hoffman
**Composition Buyer:** Linda Cox
**Manufacturing Buyer:** Megan Cochran
**Cover Designer:** Linda Knowles

This book was set in ITC Century by Denise Hoffman. It was printed and bound by Bind-Rite Graphics. The cover was printed by Phoenix Color Corporation/Hagerstown.

For Professional Development Resources visit www.allynbaconmerrill.com

**Pearson**® is a registered trademark of Pearson plc
**Merrill**® is a registered trademark of Pearson Education, Inc.

Pearson Education, Ltd.
Pearson Education Singapore Pte. Ltd.
Pearson Education Canada, Ltd.
Pearson Education–Japan

Pearson Education Australia Pty. Limited
Pearson Education North Asia Ltd.
Pearson Educacíon de Mexico, S.A. de C.V.
Pearson Education Malaysia Pte. Ltd.

**Merrill**
**is an imprint of**

**PEARSON**

www.pearsonhighered.com

10 9 8 7 6 5 4 3 2 1

ISBN 13: 978-0-205-58555-7
ISBN 10: 0-205-58555-8

I dedicate this book to my two sons, Michael and Adam,
two outstanding beginning teachers

# Contents

## Part I

## Being Inducted into the Teaching Profession: Year 1    1

## Part II

## Month-by-Month Mentoring: Reflection and Quality Discussions    11

## ● October

### Teaching for Understanding:
### Planning and Delivering Effective Instruction        63

## ● January

### Beginning a New Calendar Year: Looking Back and Moving Forward　133

## ● February

### Engaging Students in the Curriculum: Focus on Content through Active Inquiry　155

## ● March

### Collaborating with New Teachers:
### Observing and Building a Trusting Relationship     177

● June

## Completing the Year:
## Paperwork, Relationships, and Closing a Room     245

# Preface

The idea for this book came from the mentor teachers in my Mentoring in Action courses at the University of Massachusetts Dartmouth. These teachers were using the *Mentoring in Action* book successfully and they encouraged me to write a version of it for new teachers. Their rationale was that new teachers really needed to have the monthly guide at the beginning of the school year, and often mentors were not assigned in time to share the information in *Mentoring in Action: A Month-by-Month Curriculum for Mentors and Their New Teachers* (Pearson, 2006) with new teachers at the very beginning of the year. They also believe new teachers need their own copy of the book to use throughout the school year because it could serve as a documentation and reflection of that year. The seed for this idea was planted a year ago.

If you are reading this preface, you are a new teacher who has been given the book as a guide for your first year. I know you are busy; this book is not meant to add to your workload. It is designed to be used with your mentor to promote discussions that will allow you to think more deeply. If you don't have a mentor to talk to, use this book as a guide for personal self-reflection, or create your own support group with other new teachers and use it to have quality conversations about teaching.

## ● Acknowledgments

Special thanks to Steve Dragin at Pearson Education for believing that supporting new teachers makes a difference in the quality of education for students. Thank you, Karen O'Connor, for inviting me to create TEACH! SouthCoast at the Center for University, School and Community Partnerships and for reminding me to always face the sun so the shadows will fall behind me.

# Introduction
## A Letter to You the New Teacher

Dear New Teacher,

Your first year of teaching is an exciting and challenging experience. You will not only be beginning your career as a teacher, you will be building a relationship with an experienced teacher who is working with you as your mentor. This person is important to your success as a beginning teacher and your continued success in the teaching profession.

This book organizes your hectic first year so you can think about the important issues you are facing. It also serves as a tool to document conversations with your mentor or other new teachers. Keep track of your progress this year by reading the pages, writing a journal entry each month, discussing important issues listed in each chapter, reflecting at the end of each month, and setting goals for the next month. If you are required to maintain a district or state portfolio for licensing, this guide can be used to demonstrate what you have been doing each month. The completed guide at the end of the year will serve as a road map for year 2.

## ● *Why This Book?*

My hope is that this book will provide a common language and a curriculum for you and your mentor. It is not a "be all" solution, but rather just one small part of an enormously complex task of inducting new teachers into this noble profession. It is designed to be used with small groups of new teachers as well as individually if you do not have an assigned mentor from the district. Be proactive and create your own positive mentoring experience. Instead of guessing what you should be talking about each month, use this curriculum to find things that are most meaningful for you.

Your mentor may be using *Mentoring in Action: A Month-by-Month Curriculum for Mentors and Their New Teachers* (Pearson, 2006), a book I wrote for them. *Mentoring in Action* provides more specific direction for district mentors about inducting new teachers, an overview of mentoring and induction program goals, as well as an appendix that makes suggestions for busy mentors and includes 5-, 10-, 15-, 20-, 30-, and 60-minute meetings with new teachers. It also includes all the activities and pages you have here in your book. The books are designed to be used together, but can be used alone.

This book was created because both new teachers and mentors in our University of Massachusetts Dartmouth mentoring courses asked me to write a book that would mirror the *Mentoring in Action* book. Hence, *The First Year Matters: Being Mentored . . . In Action!* was born. New teachers need a practical guide and a place to write their thoughts, ideas, reflections, and to take notes for year 2.

## Why Now?

New teachers need help now. Many of you get discouraged during your first year and leave the teaching profession. This book is designed to help you through this crucial year so you will stay in this wonderfully rewarding field. Now is the time to retain quality teachers who are passionate about students.

## Why Me?

I have a passion for this work. I have been a teacher and a teacher educator for more than 35 years. I have been a public school classroom teacher for more than 20 years, a university student teaching director for 13 years, and currently I am a program director recruiting new teachers for urban districts. In that role for the federally funded Transition to Teaching TEACH! SouthCoast program, I work with new teachers regularly. I hear their issues; I see their needs. My visits to schools have shown me that new teachers are incredibly busy and are moving in so many directions that often the most obvious skills are not being discussed. Problems take center stage and talking about one student's behavior often dominates mentoring conversations. This book frames the year so that more curriculum-based topics are discussed in a more systematic way. This doesn't mean that problems are not discussed with your mentor, they are just not *the only thing* you need to focus on while being mentored.

## Why You?

You are reading this book because the district gave it to you or because you found the book on your own and chose to read it. Either way, you are the key to a successful mentoring and induction program. If you are not fully engaged, it doesn't matter how many resources the district offers you.

I hope you will find inspiration and motivation in the pages of this book to support you as you begin an incredible year of learning. Use your vitality and positive energy to affect the students in your classrooms and share your energy freely.

May you find joy in this work during your first learning year and may you find commitment to this profession for many years to come.

Sincerely,

*Carol Pelletier Radford*

Carol Pelletier Radford, Ed.D.
Program Director
TEACH! SouthCoast
Center for University, School & Community Partnerships
University of Massachusetts Dartmouth

# Being Inducted into the Teaching Profession

## Year 1

Schools and districts are expected to provide high-quality induction for you as a new teacher entering the teaching profession because retaining high-quality teachers has become a priority in the United States. Based on a report of the National Commission on Teaching and America's Future (2003), 50 percent of the new teachers hired are leaving before their fifth year of teaching. Researchers are asking why, and are getting a variety of responses. You may be asked why you chose teaching, but you probably are not thinking about why you would stay. You are just trying to get through your first year. Induction is going to be part of your transition into teaching. So what *is* induction and how will you know if you are in a *program*?

## What Is Induction?

If you ask different people you will get different answers because there are several ways to define induction. Induction is defined in the *Merriam-Webster Dictionary* as: **1a** the act or process of inducting (as into office); **b** an initial experience; **c** the formality by which a civilian is inducted into military service. Most people think of military induction **c**, and many teachers don't like the term *induction* for that reason and prefer to use *mentoring* instead. This leads to confusion about what induction actually is, because mentoring is just one of the components of an effective induction program.

We would agree then that **b**, an initial experience, applies to new teachers who are entering teaching for the very first time. New teachers will have an "initial experience" by nature of just being in teaching their first year. Whether the experience is positive or negative is another question. "An initial experience," however, still doesn't describe *what* induction actually is. Many articles have been written about induction and mentoring, but in my opinion the leading institution in the area of teacher induction is The New Teacher Center at the University of Santa Cruz in California. This center has been developing models for new teachers and mentors for almost two decades, and serves as a model for both research and practice. Although it offers all of us practical ideas, inspiration, and research-based studies to improve the work of induction, its leader, Ellen Moir, continues to expand the vision to bring more teachers the induction support they need to survive in twenty-first-century classrooms.

Based on my reading, talking with mentors, and interacting with school districts, I believe we need several key components to create successful high-quality induction programs. You may add your own, but the lesson here is that there are several components to induction, not just mentoring. The components I suggest are a clear plan for the program, resources, orientations throughout the school year, mentoring (one-on-one or small groups), professional development, and a program evaluation to determine whether teachers actually felt supported by the program. The larger research question, "Do new teachers stay in teaching?" is an important one for school districts right now because so many teachers are leaving. Another question for us all to consider is: Why are new teachers leaving?

This guide is designed for you to be able to reflect on and discuss your first year in an organized way. Because we all know it will be hectic and uncertain, it is important to be proactive and to provide you with a tool that is easy to use and that is organized around the school year. Use this guide to reflect on why you will stay for a second year.

## ● *A Plan for Induction*

Districts may have an induction committee or advisory board to design what the new teachers entering the district may need to be successful. Induction should go beyond the first year because it takes several years to "become" a teacher. Are you aware of the plan in your district? Do you have to complete requirements either for the district or the state license related to induction? Some new teachers ask in their interviews if they will be assigned a mentor. Having a mentor is one component of a high-quality induction program.

## ● *Resources*

It costs money to organize a new-teacher induction program. Several states have mandated school districts provide induction and mentoring, but they have not funded these mandates. Unfunded mandates cause financial pressure in districts because the money has to be taken from other internal budgets. Schools need all their resources for teaching students and are challenged to stretch the finances further, so induction and mentoring sometimes are limited to paper plans with little real formal implementation. Is the induction program in your district funded? Did someone buy you this book?

## ● *Orientations*

As a new teacher beginning your teaching you will have lots of nuts-and-bolts-type questions that relate to health insurance, taxes, evaluation, and union dues. These questions are usually answered at district orientations that are scheduled prior to the first days of school. Districts with financial resources may hire their district mentors also to orient the new teachers to the school and the district. Most districts do this as large group meetings with small breakouts by school or department. These orientations are important because they relate to your survival needs. Where do I do the copying? Where do I pick up my paycheck? How do I get supplies? Does your district have scheduled orientations to answer these types of questions? How will you get your questions answered?

## Professional Development

Induction programs need professional development for both the new teachers and their mentor/facilitators. District needs, new-teacher needs, and mentor needs should all be considered. Ultimately, all the professional development should relate to student learning. New teachers like you consistently have stated they need more information and training in teaching the district curriculum. Experts also know new teachers also need more ideas and support with classroom management, time management, and pacing lessons and units, as well as behavior management and discipline. I am sure you are looking forward to these discussions. Make sure you review the Contents in this guide to get some practical ideas for these topics. They are offered each month, but you may go ahead and read them all at once to get an overview.

## Program Evaluation

The evaluation of an induction program will let the district know how successful they have been in meeting your needs as a new teacher. Make sure you give input to the leaders in the school district so they know what they are doing right and where they could enhance their support for you. Your mentor can assist you in providing feedback to the district.

## Mentoring

You will hopefully be assigned a formal mentor who will work with you throughout the school year using this guide as a framework for discussion and reflection. Sometimes assigning a mentor to a new teacher is considered an "induction" program. The other components previously mentioned are either not funded or are not included in the vision for assisting new teachers, perhaps because this is all the district can afford or because there is little understanding of the variety of components of induction. Having a mentor as the sole provider of support for you puts enormous pressure on one person who is usually teaching full time. Think about a variety of ways in which you can get support.

I support the concept of group mentoring because, in my experience, new teachers benefit by listening to other new teachers. This *group mentoring* concept puts the mentor teacher in the role of *facilitator* and perhaps even the role of *teacher of new teachers*, rather than the idealized role of mentor imparting information or questions to one person who solves them on his or her own. This guide provides a sample agenda for group mentoring discussions each month. If your district does not offer a formal support group, be proactive and create one for yourself! Both one-on-one and group mentoring are important to the success of an induction program.

## Building a Relationship with Your Mentor

Districts and schools may have job descriptions for their mentors depending upon union contracts and state mandates for mentoring. Ask your mentor what his or her role is in supporting you so you know what to expect and what you will not be receiving for support. Ask if you will be observed or if you can observe your mentor in action.

If you want to get the most out of a mentoring experience, it is important to know your mentor. Use the following Relationship Profile as a guide to discover who you are and what you believe. You don't have to copy your mentor's style. Notice how you are different and how you are alike. Use your discussions to deepen your understanding of each other and why you choose to teach in certain ways.

Acknowledging your diverse perspectives and respecting these differences publicly promotes a trusting relationship. This is one way to build a relationship with your mentor. Confidentiality is critical to trust. How will you keep your mentor's conversations and perspectives confidential?

## INTASC Principles and How They Relate to You

If your mentor is using the companion guide, *Mentoring in Action: A Month-by-Month Curriculum for Mentors and Their New Teachers*, you can both map out your year on a monthly calendar and set up times to discuss how your students are learning. Review the Interstate New Teachers Assessment and Support Consortium (INTASC) principles (page 14) and discuss how they relate to your ability to teach your students.

## Being Mentored *in ACTION:* What Does That Mean?

This guide is titled *The First Year Matters: Being Mentored . . . In Action!*, because as a new teacher you will be "in action" when you are using this book. The first year does matter. How you begin your career as a teacher makes a difference in your attitude and your ability to view the profession in a positive way. Many new teachers have a *sink-or-swim* induction program—no mentor, no support, no guidebook like this—and they have had difficult experiences.

One activity I have been doing with new teachers for years empowers them to *create* their own board of mentors. The idea for this process came to me when I was sitting in a workshop led by Karma B. Kitaj. (You can find out more about her work at www.lifespringcoaching.com.) She had me think about my own mentors who helped me and I developed this process for you. As a new teacher, you will need many different kinds of support, some emotional, some related to curriculum, and perhaps social support, too. Use Your Board of Mentors Worksheet on page 7 to acknowledge who you will turn to this year when you need help.

Use the space below to brainstorm a list of people in your life who have helped you in some way. Some of the people on your list may have passed on but you find comfort in the wise things they shared with you about life. Think about "how" you use each of the people on your list. For example, I turn to my brother Jim if I need advice about finances because he is an accountant; I turn to my friend Nancy when I need encouragement about relationships.

# The Relationship Profile

**Directions:** Through informal conversations, ACTs listed in each month, planned discussions, or an interview, complete the table to find out where your mentor and you are alike and different. Feel free to add your own columns to the table. What would you like to know about each other?

| Topics | Philosophy of Teaching *What do we believe?* *Why did we choose teaching?* *Will we teach for a career?* | Career Stage and Age *How do we compare?* *What are our life issues?* *What is happening in our lives right now?* *How does it affect teaching and mentoring?* | Teaching and Learning Styles *How do we teach and how do we like to learn?* *How do we like to get feedback?* | Personality and Life Goals *How do we interact with others?* *What are our priorities in life?* |
|---|---|---|---|---|
| New teacher | | First year! Age: Could be 22 or 52! | | |
| Mentor | | How old? How many years as a mentor? How many years as a teacher? How many schools? | | |
| Similarities and differences; what shows up | | | | |

**Directions for Your Board of Mentors Worksheet:** Print your name at the head of the table sitting in the chair and write *self-reflection* on the line above your chair. Your role this year is to reflect on what is happening and use your reflections to forward your teaching practice. Now write a name in each chair, selecting from the list on page 5. Be sure to write the way this person supports you on the line. Include your district mentor in one of the chairs. Add more chairs to your table if you need them.

Name _____     Date _____

## Your Board of Mentors

### ● New-Teacher Support Groups

One-on-one mentoring can be expensive and some districts just can't afford it. Release time, substitutes, mentor training, matching, and providing resources for each new teacher separately may not be the only way to provide induction support. As previously discussed in the beginning of this section, it makes sense to work in small mentor-facilitated groups and new teachers often like it. This doesn't mean all mentoring should be done in groups! Even though many new teachers prefer to work in small groups there will be time when you need one-on-one conversations with a confidential colleague. If you do not have an assigned mentor, seek out a colleague or meet with the principal to discuss your needs. Everyone wants you to succeed. Don't wait until the end of the year to say you didn't receive the support you needed. Act now. Use the pages in this book each month to organize productive sharing sessions.

### ● Creating Opportunities for Quality Conversations

This guide is all about creating opportunities for quality conversations. In fact, it goes beyond informal conversation to discussions that are formal and rich in the opportunity they bring both to you and to your mentor. Mentoring does not mean talking *at* you, but sometimes mentors are so enthusiastic they want to tell you everything to save you from the first-year pitfalls. They do this with compassion and empathy, and sometimes without thinking that this might not be the best way for you to embrace the initial year of teaching.

Discussion and communication implies that there is talking and listening going on. Because mentors have all the information they believe you need, they tend to talk and tell. Some mentors will say, "I ask the new teachers what they need and they say they don't know, so I tell them." This may be the case for you, so be patient with your mentor.

The key is to balance the talking and the listening so you have an entry point into the conversation or discussion. Sometimes writing works for new teachers. Using the REFLECTions at the end of each chapter may provide an opportunity for you to share what you are thinking and what you need to be successful. See if you can insert your ideas and thoughts into mentoring conversations professionally.

### ● Do You Really Listen?

How many times have we all been able to do three things at the same time? Sometimes we are talking and we don't even know what we are saying to the other person! Setting up times to talk with your mentor when you are free of interruption will be a challenge, but one that is well worth your time and effort. A 10-minute meeting that is focused and during which you are able to listen will be more useful to you than a 30-minute session when your mind is on correcting papers.

Know the difference between a short conversation about something specific and an in-depth discussion related to student learning or a topic of choice. This guide encourages you to make time for these discussions, where you can really listen and make eye contact with your mentor. Just *stop* what you are doing and listen to yourself and to your mentor. That is a *quality conversation* that enhances mentoring.

Ask yourself: Am I really listening, or am I thinking about what I want to say next? Both new teachers and mentors need to be active listeners, who don't judge, preach, or lecture. What are some barriers to listening actively?

If you assume you know what your mentor is going to say, you probably are not actively listening.

If you are easily distracted and can't maintain eye contact, you probably are not actively listening.

If you draw a conclusion before your mentor is finished, you probably are not actively listening.

If you are daydreaming or writing your shopping list, you probably are not actively listening.

If you are tired, you probably are not actively listening.

What other barriers can you think of? How will you overcome the barriers to listening so you can get the most out of mentoring conversations?

## ● *Participating in Ongoing Reflection*

An area that often gets dropped from very busy schedules is reflection. Who has time? It sounds like a good idea, but it just never seems to fit. This guide includes two easy forms of reflection. The first is at the beginning of the month and is a *journal entry*. It allows you to write whatever you are feeling at the time. It may be shared with your mentor or you may want to keep it private, a record of your thoughts and feelings that day. A second form of reflection that is quick and easy for you to complete is designed for the end of the month. The *reflection bubbles* have one short prompt in each of them that is designed to elicit a short response. The responses can be discussed later or just saved as reminders of what you would like to discuss with your mentor at the end of the month. If your mentor is using the *Mentoring in Action* guide, he or she will have his or her own bubble prompts to share with you or other mentors.

Another way to reflect is to use a *dialogue journal*. This allows you and your mentor to communicate and reflect while writing back and forth. Hard-copy journals can be kept in a mutually convenient place. One person starts the conversation and the other writes back. This is a quick and easy way to answer questions during the school day if the mentor is in your building. No one has to be interrupted, and the answer to your question will be in the dialogue journal at the end of the day. Of course, email provides an easy alternative to the dialogue journal. The chats could go beyond one-on-one; all new teachers could participate reflecting on a topic in a chatroom or other platform.

### ● *Maintaining a Professional Community of Learners*

This guide is really about creating a professional community with your mentor and other new teachers. If you are the only new teacher entering the school, then you will have to work with your mentor to reach out to other colleagues who may not be new teachers. Your mentor can teach you about collegiality with the more experienced teachers and assist you in sharing ideas.

Teaching is also part of a wider professional community that includes professional organizations and teacher unions. You will want to be included in district organizations as well as the teacher union. Professional organizations also offer journals, conferences, and materials that can enhance your experiences during your first year of teaching.

Holding new-teacher support groups, creating opportunities for quality conversations, participating in ongoing reflection, listening, and maintaining a professional community of learners are all part of being mentored. Read each of the following sections in this book and think seriously about how you can integrate these important ideas into your framework for teaching and learning.

This collaborative guide offers a road map for the mentoring discussion journey that can assist you in knowing what to talk about, but it doesn't have all the answers. You already know that there will be detours along the way. That's the nature of the work. Staying with the process, and being "in action" with your district mentor, your board of mentors, and the new teachers in your support group means you will be responding to your own needs as you go. Enjoy the ride.

# Part II

## Month-by-Month Mentoring
### Reflection and Quality Discussions

## Why Do We Need a Mentoring Curriculum?

Some mentoring programs simply assign a mentor to a new teacher at the beginning of the year and say, "Go mentor." They know the experienced teacher is a good classroom teacher who wants to help a new teacher; the question is, are they good at working with a new teacher? You may be working with a new mentor who has never done this before, or you could be working with a teacher who has formally or informally mentored hundreds of new teachers. It doesn't matter in which situation you find yourself. A mentoring curriculum can assist in focusing discussions to maximize your time.

As with your students, you need to write the daily agenda on the board. Students need to know where they are headed. This curriculum does that for you. It is an outline of a typical year, organized by months, because teachers' lives are organized by months, terms, and semesters. Most activities fall into certain times of the year and you need to know when to expect them. This curriculum won't fit your situation exactly, and that is why you need to review the entire year so you can skip around to meet your own needs. Your mentor will also be able to guide you so that you are reading and reviewing pages that make most sense each month. Remember this is a *guide*, not a script. You are in control of how this curriculum will work best in your teaching context.

Mentors often start off strong in August or September and work with you to get the new year started. Often the relationship gets less formal as the year goes on and, by the end of the year, you may find yourself on your own. With a guide like this, you can refer to certain pages and months and use it to ask your mentor or other teachers questions about topics that you find unfamiliar. This book is designed to reduce your anxiety, because you will know what is coming and will have a list of topics that will enhance your teaching success all year, not just at the beginning. Pay particular attention to May and June so you can get the help you need in closing out your school year.

## A Month-by-Month Framework
## for Reflection and Discussions

You can't learn everything at once. Be kind to yourself. This is a new experience. Skim the table of contents and the months at the beginning of this book so you are familiar with what is here, and notice if there is anything you need to read right now. It is OK to skip around and do what works for you. With a curriculum, it is ensured that we touch on the important topics. Reflection on your practice and what you are thinking should be written on the pages in this book so you can review them with your mentor monthly and at the end of the school year as well.

You will notice that for each month there is a topic that is a focus for that month. There are also some recurring topics each month. They repeat, because new teachers have said that they need more discussions of classroom management and communication with parents. Teaching is complex work that needs to be teased apart to analyze and discuss.

Each chapter contains repeating pages that are in the same order each month. The month always begins with a cover page that includes the particular feature pictured here to focus your attention and to provide a context for the discussions. The cover page is followed by a one-page narrative and space for a journal entry. Sample questions you may ask your mentor or other teachers, and sample questions to expect from your mentor are included here as well. Check the ones that apply to you.

The mantra for this guide is PLAN, CONNECT, ACT, REFLECT, and SET GOALS. These are concrete, consistent, practical terms that will engage you and your mentor in having quality discussions and reflection. They can become natural and systematic. Each verb adds an "action" for being mentored in action and provides an array of options from which to choose. You don't need to do them all. Just one will integrate the term and will keep you PLANning, CONNECTing, completing ACTivities, REFLECTing, and SETting GOALS. This is an important routine and skill set for you to learn. You may apply this to your lesson plans with your students, too! Use these pages like you would a personal journal. Write in them, scribble, doodle, make notes, add sticky notes, and save them for future reference.

# Mentoring in Action

## Month-by-Month Mentoring

### August

**Orientation to the School and Community**

Space, Procedures, Resources, Values, and Culture

### September

**Brginning the School Year Successfully**

Creating a Community of Learners in the Classroom

### October

**Teaching for Understanding**

Planning and Delivering Effective Instruction

### November

**Assessing Diverse Learners**

How Do Teachers Know Students Have Learned?

### December

**Maintaining Balance**

Teaching and Keeping the Students Interested

### January

**Beginning a New Calendar Year**

Looking Back and Moving Forward

### February
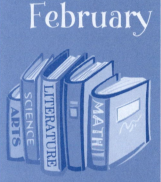
**Engaging Students in the Curriculum**

Focus on Content through Active Inquiry

### March

**Collaborating with New Teachers**

Observing and Building a Trusting Relationship

### April

**Standards**

Creating Meaningful Standards-Based Learning Experiences for Students

### May

**Assessing Students' Progress**

High-Stakes Tests and Teacher Assessment

### June
**Completing the Year**

Paperwork, Relationships, and Closing a Room

# INTASC Principles

## Interstate New Teachers Assessment and Support Consortium

● **Principle 1   Making Content Meaningful**
The teacher understands the central concepts, tools of inquiry, and structures of the disciplines he or she teaches and creates learning experiences that make these aspects of subject matter meaningful for students.

● **Principle 2   Child Development and Learning Theory**
The teacher understands how children learn and develop, and can provide learning opportunities that support their intellectual, social, and personal development.

● **Principle 3   Learning Styles/Diversity**
The teacher understands how students differ in their approaches to learning and creates instructional opportunities that are adapted to diverse learners.

● **Principle 4   Instructional Strategies/Problem Solving**
The teacher understands and uses a variety of instructional strategies to encourage students' development of critical thinking, problem solving, and performance skills.

● **Principle 5   Motivation and Behavior**
The teacher uses an understanding of individual and group motivation and behavior to create a learning environment that encourages positive social interaction, active engagements in learning, and self-motivation.

● **Principle 6   Communication/Knowledge**
The teacher uses knowledge of effective verbal, nonverbal, and media communication techniques to foster active inquiry, collaboration, and supportive interaction in the classroom.

● **Principle 7   Planning for Instruction**
The teacher plans instruction based upon knowledge of subject matter, students, the community, and curriculum goals.

● **Principle 8   Assessment**
The teacher understands and uses formal and informal assessment strategies to evaluate and ensure the continuous intellectual, social, and physical development of the learner.

● **Principle 9   Professional Growth/Reflection**
The teacher is a reflective practitioner who continually evaluates the effects of his or her choices and actions on others (students, parents, and other professionals in the learning community) and who actively seeks out opportunities to grow professionally.

● **Principle 10   Interpersonal Relationships**
The teacher fosters relationships with school colleagues, parents, and agencies in the larger community to support students' learning and well-being.

*Source:* http://cte.jhu.edu/pds/resources/intasc_principles.htm

*Good teachers care about their students, know who they are, and would go to any length to help them get the education they deserve.* —High School Student

# Orientation to the School and Community
## Space, Procedures, Resources, Values, and Culture

**New-Teacher Phase:** Anticipation

*"I'm so excited to have my own classroom!"*

## INTASC Principles

Review INTASC Principles 1 through 10. A complete list is available on page 14 in Part II. Each month, one or two principles will be reviewed in more depth to ensure all principles are discussed in your first year. District evaluation standards should also be reviewed throughout the school year and should be compared with INTASC Principles. Ask your mentor to share district expectations with you.

## Orientation to the School and Community
### Space, Procedures, Resources, Values, and Culture

Being mentored while you are in your first classroom is both exciting and exhausting work. This guide, *The First Year Mattters: Being Mentored . . . In Action!* will provide you with a framework for discussions with your new colleagues. Depending upon your district, your mentoring program may vary. Do you have a mentor assigned to assist you? If you don't, use this book as a way to reflect on what you are doing and share it with other new teachers.

You may feel isolated and alone right now. Document your journey into teaching by completing the pages in this book as you go through the school year. If you do have a district mentor, use the pages in this book to frame your discussions so you don't waste valuable time. This book is also designed to be used in a new-teacher support group, or as a personal journal to capture your thoughts throughout the year.

August is an opportunity for you to meet other new teachers in the school and the community. Who are the other new teachers? Who are the students? What are their cultures? What does the school value? What is the mission statement for the school and do teachers, students, parents, and administrators honor it?

Create a *survival guide* for yourself (see the ACTions pages this month) and discuss it with other new teachers. You will soon discover that there is a lot more to teaching than preparing lessons. Even though you are excited to be in your first classroom, you may not fully understand or know your school procedures. Be patient, be resourceful, and ask questions so you can get organized. Beginning in August, before the students arrive, is a plus to any teacher mentoring program, so use this time to your advantage. Skim through the entire book so you will know how it is organized and what it includes for discussion topics each month. Feel free to pick and choose activities that relate to your experience this month.

## ● Journal Entry

**Directions:** Read the cover page and the narrative for this month. How does this month's topic, the quotes, phase, and narrative overview relate to you right now? Are you comfortable with this topic? Do you need some help? How are you feeling right now?

Use your journal to record your thoughts, feelings, and questions in a free-flowing narrative. This page is for your personal reflection; it does not need to be shared as a written document. You are, however, encouraged to share excerpts with other new teachers or with your mentor as needed.

### Reflections:

*Today . . .*

Date _____

## ● PLAN Being Mentored . . . In Action!
### *Questions for Participating in a Quality Conversation*

Participating in a mentoring conversation requires you to be fully engaged. It requires listening and being open to what your mentor is sharing. This means you need to think about the questions you have and how to ask them. It does not mean you have to copy exactly what your mentor recommends, but it does mean you will reflect on the conversations and think about what makes sense for you.

Other new teachers have had these questions in August. Check the questions that you would like to discuss with your mentor or other new teachers in your school or district.

### New Teachers' Possible Questions:

\_\_\_\_ How do I create a community of learners? What does that look like?

\_\_\_\_ Who are my students and their families?

\_\_\_\_ What do I need to know about the community?

\_\_\_\_ What do I need to know about this school and its procedures for opening a school year and a new classroom?

\_\_\_\_ What values, expectations, or cultural norms are in operation in this school and the community?

\_\_\_\_ Is there a written mission statement for the school?

\_\_\_\_ Do you have any suggestions for me as I set up my first classroom?

\_\_\_\_ How do I get materials for my classroom and my students?

\_\_\_\_ Are there any restrictions or expectations for setting up my classroom space?

\_\_\_\_ Other questions I have . . .

## ● Be Prepared
### *Your Mentor May Also Ask You Questions!*

### Mentor's Possible Questions:

\_\_\_\_ What do you already know about this community?

\_\_\_\_ What are you planning to do to prepare your room and why are you doing that?

\_\_\_\_ Do you have any experience setting up a classroom?

\_\_\_\_ What can I do to assist you right now that would reduce your anxiety?

## ● Monthly Organizer

### *What I Need to Do Each Month*

**Orientation to the School and Community:**
**Space, Procedures, Resources, Values, and Culture**

| *Pages in this month's chapter help me to . . .* | | |
|---|---|---|
| **PLAN** | Read the title page quotes and standards | page 15 |
| | Read the narrative page | page 16 |
| | Read "Plan Your Time Wisely" | page 20 |
| | Complete the calendar with meeting dates | page 21 |
| **CONNECT** | Review connections | page 22 |
| | Connect with other new teachers | page 22 |
| **ACT** | Review the list of choices | page 23 |
| | Complete the pages you selected | pages 24–36 |
| **REFLECT** | Complete your journal entry | page 17 |
| | Fill in the bubbles | page 37 |
| **SET GOALS** | What's next for you? | page 38 |

## • PLAN Your Time Wisely

### What Is Important to You?

The beginning of the school year is hectic. You may have just been hired and you haven't even met your mentor yet. As a new teacher, you will quickly discover you don't seem to have enough time to do all you need to do. It is important for you to be proactive and schedule meetings when you need them. There will be meetings scheduled at the school that are required and others that are optional. Assess which meetings will support you. Planning your time wisely is crucial to your success in the classroom. Schedule meetings with your mentor and your support group of new teachers first. Make being mentored in action a priority each month.

### Location and Time for Meetings

Use the key at the bottom of the calendar page to indicate the time of your meeting and place it on the calendar along with the time, length of meeting, and location. Select a private location for meetings with your mentor or colleagues. Make sure you select a place where you will not be interrupted. Meetings may range from five minutes to an hour! What works for you will depend on what you need and what the focus of the meeting is for that day.

### Being Proactive

To be mentored in action means you need to be thinking about what you need as you are doing your work as a teacher. Sometimes this can be confusing and difficult at best. Use your skills and intuition to guide you regarding what you need and when. Then be proactive in *asking* for help. This does not mean you are incompetent. Sometimes new teachers feel they don't want to bother other adults in the school and that they can wait until a formal meeting is held before they ask for help. Most experienced teachers don't mind setting aside time to answer a few questions, and the answers to these questions could alleviate a lot of stress.

### Anticipate

Schedule a few short meetings when you think you might need them. Anticipate the days or times that would be most useful to you. For example, at the end of the week you may have lots of questions, as opposed to the beginning of the week, when you don't really know what to ask yet. Use August to schedule some time with experienced people in the district even if they are not your official mentor. What do you have to lose? Nothing. And if you meet and you don't have any questions, you can just enjoy each other's company!

# August Calendar

| MONDAY | TUESDAY | WEDNESDAY | THURSDAY | FRIDAY |
|--------|---------|-----------|----------|--------|
|        |         |           |          |        |
|        |         |           |          |        |
|        |         |           |          |        |
|        |         |           |          |        |
|        |         |           |          |        |

Key: B = Before school  D = During the day (preparation time or lunchtime)  A = After school

## ● CONNECT with People, Readings, Professional Associations, Resources, and Technology

▶ *What are the resources that exist in your school and community that could assist you in setting up your first classroom?*

**Directions:**

1. Review your journal entry and questions from the *PLAN Being Mentored . . . In Action!* page for this month.

2. How can you *connect* with people in your school or district, readings, professional associations, resources, or technology to help you? You may complete this page by yourself, with your mentor, or with a group of new teachers.

### CONNECT *with People . . .*

Who in the school building (experienced teachers, other beginning teachers, custodians, secretaries, etc.) may be able to help with August needs?

Who or what agency in the community could provide resources or support for free or low cost?

How can parents be helpful in setting up a classroom and what are the protocols for inviting them in?

**Names:**

### CONNECT *with Readings, Professional Associations, and Resources . . .*

What have you read or used that could assist you in setting up your first classroom? Don't forget to use your student teaching courses and materials to help you. Get them out of those boxes. Your mentors or school district may also have free books and materials for first-year teachers. Just ask!

**Titles:**

### CONNECT *with Technology . . .*

Find websites and links that will provide information about

- The district and community
- The school
- Students and parents
- How to set up a first classroom (search by *elementary* or *secondary*)
- First day and week activities (search by *elementary* or *secondary*)

**Websites:**

## ● ACTIVITIES: Select Topics for Reflection and Discussion

### *How Do I Begin the Year?*

This is the beginning of your first teaching experience and you are both excited and nervous. Use this chapter as a guide to start your year off on a positive note. This list of activities requires you to ACT either by reflecting on a topic or discussing the topic with your mentor, other experienced teachers, or other new teachers. These activities are designed to stimulate your thinking. Write in this book so you will have a documentation of your thoughts and ideas for next year's planning. You do not have to complete all activities.

## Orientation to the School and Community:
## Space, Procedures, Resources, Values, and Culture

| **FIRST STEP:** Start the month by organizing a new-teacher support group! | | |
|---|---|---|
| ✓ | **Check the ACTivities from the following list that are most meaningful for you to discuss.** | **Page** |
| | ACT 1    What Do You Bring to Teaching? | 26 |
| | ACT 2    Getting to Know Your Mentor | 27 |
| | ACT 3    Goals and Expectations for the Mentoring Experience | 28 |
| | ACT 4    Orientation to the School and District: Meeting Important People | 29 |
| | ACT 5    Orientation to the Students and Their Families in the Community | 30 |
| | ACT 6    Being Mentored | 31 |
| | ACT 7    Creating a Survival Packet: What You Need to Know Now | 32 |
| | ACT 8    The First Days and Weeks of School | 33 |
| | ACT 9    Other Support Systems for New Teachers: University Connections | 34 |
| | ACT 10   District Evaluation and Support Groups | 35 |
| | ACT 11   New-Teacher Needs | 36 |

## ● FIRST STEP:  Create a New-Teacher Support Group

You will probably attend a district orientation this month. Many times this is a host of introductions, medical insurance forms, and listening to district programs. In excellent programs you will have an opportunity to meet your mentor, set up your classroom, and meet the other new teachers in the district. If this is not the case for you, then be professionally proactive and ask the administration in the district if you can meet with other new teachers after the orientation agenda is complete. This topic of learning about your school and community is important. Make sure you discover as much as you can as you begin your year.

Here are some tips for hosting a successful monthly support group:

- Work with district mentors to find a comfortable place to meet after school. You may decide to meet in a classroom. After school is better for these meetings, because you will not need to rush to class and complete your morning duties.

- Have refreshments and perhaps even some music playing as teachers enter the room.

- Follow an agenda so those who attend know they are not wasting their time. The topic for each month in this book is a good place to start and focus. There is so much involved in teaching that it is easy to get sidetracked. There is an agenda in each chapter located after the ACTion pages list. Use this as a guide.

- Post a sign on the room that says, "Meeting in Progress. Please come back at [XX time]" to avoid interruptions.

- Invite other teachers in the building who want to share ideas too.

- Don't make this a gripe session. Keep the meeting in the problem-solving mode with ideas and suggestions shared by the group.

- Set talking ground rules so everyone gets to share. For example, everyone talks once before someone talks a second time.

- Assign a time keeper.

- Set the next meeting date. Try to host the meetings in as many classrooms as possible. This allows your group to see other classroom organizations and materials.

## Notes

How will I set up a group?

Who do I want to include?

Questions I have about organizing a group:

    Ask my mentor . . .

    Ask other new teachers . . .

    Ask administrators . . .

Idea to share at first meeting . . .

## What Do You Bring to Teaching?

Do you bring energy, passion, and new ideas to this profession? Are you excited about becoming a teacher? Use the New-Teacher Profile to reflect on your journey into teaching and how you arrived here. Use additional paper to respond to these questions. Share this profile with your mentor and other new teachers in your new-teacher support group.

**New-Teacher Profile**

I. *Teacher Preparation*

    A. Describe your preparation for teaching as defined in your course work. Describe the course that stands out for you as one that has prepared you and why. Highlight your content knowledge as well as your methods courses on your transcript.

    B. List your previous experiences in schools as a student teacher or previous work with young children or adolescents.

II. *Skills and Experiences*

    A. Do you speak another language? Explain.

    B. Do you or have you played or coached sports? Explain.

    C. Where have you traveled? Why did you visit these places?

    D. Do you have musical, drama, or any arts ability? Explain.

    E. What is your level of proficiency with computers and other technology?

    F. What are your hobbies?

III. *Life Goals*

    A. Where do you see yourself in five years? Ten years? Twenty years?

    B. Why did you choose teaching?

IV. *Personal Joys*

    A. What gives you joy?

    B. What would you like others to know about you?

## Getting to Know Your Mentor

This relationship can be one that is both personal and professional. Because you will be sharing your challenges and successes with your mentor, you will want to build a relationship of trust. Use the relationship profile on page 6 to guide you in learning how you are alike and how you are different. The goal of mentoring is not to make you a clone of your mentor. It is to assist you in discovering your own style and using your strengths.

Interview your mentor. Sample questions include the following:

1. How many years have you been teaching? In this area? At this school?

2. Why did you become a teacher? A mentor teacher?

3. What do you see as the strengths of my class/school/community?

4. What will your expectations be for me?

5. How can I assist you in creating a positive mentoring experience?

## Goals and Expectations
## for the Mentoring Experience

1. List your own personal goals for this experience:

   a. _____

   b. _____

   c. _____

2. I expect to

   a. _____

   b. _____

   c. _____

3. Verify your expectations with your mentor to avoid confusion. What does the district expect from you as a new teacher?

   _____

   _____

   _____

   _____

Share your expectations with your mentor. Ask your mentor to share his or her job description. Make sure you are clear what your mentor will and will not do. Your mentor usually is not going to evaluate you for rehiring, but you need to be sure what her or his role is so you can understand how to participate in this relationship.

*Reflection:*

Were there any areas that you expected that are not going to be met through mentoring?

_____

_____

If yes, how will you have these needs met?

_____

_____

_____

# Orientation to the School and District: Meeting Important People

Introduce yourself to other professionals as you meet them:

- Principals and headmasters as well as assistants who were not part of the interview
- Department chairs who were not part of the interview
- Teachers in the building by grade level and department
- Specialist teachers (art, music, computer, physical education, etc.)
- Bilingual teachers
- Support specialists (guidance, clinical psychologist, nurse, physical therapy)
- Special education teachers (share the model your school is using—inclusion or pull-out)
- Support personnel (secretaries, aides, paraprofessionals)
- Custodians and lunchroom employees
- Parents (volunteer groups or formally organized groups)
- Building-based support teams
- Police officers

Ask for a complete list of personnel so you have the correct spelling of their names!

### School Scavenger Hunt (complete with other new teachers)

Invite the new teachers to find these answers before the next meeting. They can use the school district website or background information you provide as well as interview with the people listed earlier.

1. Complete name of the school and why it has this name. Age of the school. Also, attach phone, email, website address, and directions to the school with a local map.
2. How many students are enrolled in this school? What is the diversity of students by ethnicity? The languages spoken? The ages of students by grade level?
3. What are the school hours? When are recesses? Lunches? What are the schedules? Are they blocks?
4. Is public transportation available? If so, what is the schedule?
5. What is the theme or mission of the school? How is it portrayed?
6. How are the classrooms organized? Number? Size? Shape of school? Number of teachers per grade level?
7. What is the profile of the teachers by years of experience? Are any teachers bilingual? Multilingual?
8. Are there special programs or activities in this school?
9. What are the teachers the most proud of in this school?
10. How does this school relate to other schools in the district?

## Orientation to the Students and Their Families in the Community

Getting to know the students and the local community is important, especially if you have moved from another city or state. Here are a few ideas for getting acquainted with students and their families:

1. *Interview students.*  Meet with a few students at the school before the school year begins, if possible. They do not have to be students in your classes; pick any student who is willing to talk with a new teacher. Ask the students what they like and don't like about the school.

2. *Interview parents.*  Ask the parents to share how they work with teachers in this school. What do they like and dislike about this school?

3. *Take a tour of the community.*  Many school districts provide a tour to new teachers. If there is not one in your district, take a bus or drive around to all the neighborhoods where students live who attend your school. Where are the town landmarks—the library, the YMCA, and so forth?

4. *Review the school district website.*  Read and review the website for important information about the school and the community.

5. Discuss this information with your mentor.

## Being Mentored

What do you think your role is with regard to being mentored?

_____

_____

_____

_____

_____

_____

_____

_____

_____

_____

You can get the most out of being mentored by . . .

*Asking questions* (by email, phone, using a dialogue journal, or in person). A dialogue journal is a book that is placed in the mentor's classroom. If you have a question, write it in the journal and when the mentor has a minute, she or he responds. The next time you come in to the room, read the response and write back. This works because it allows both of you to write when you have a chance. Also, all the questions will be in writing to review at the end of the year. Quick and easy!

*Visiting* the mentor's classroom before or after school on a regular basis. Getting to know the systems, routines, and students in another classroom will allow you to see that some of the issues you face are the same for your mentor. All teachers face misbehavior issues and how to handle mounds of paper work!

*Making time* to meet with your mentor or other new teachers. Time is the essential ingredient for success through reflection. Using this guide will provide the structure for formal discussions, but you have to see these discussions as important. You have to make time to reflect on and solve your own issues.

August

## Creating a Survival Packet:
## What You Need to Know Now

Collect as many materials listed below and organize them in a binder labeled *Survival Tips*.

I. Materials
  A. Schedules (daily, weekly, block, holiday)
  B. Student and school handbooks with policies
  C. Mission statements and vision statements
  D. Curriculum guides for grade levels
  E. List of faculty with phone numbers
  F. Class lists
  G. Report cards and parent communication
  H. Discipline policies
  I. Professional development schedule
  J. State policy for reporting abuse, neglect, or other legal issues

II. Buzz Words (here is a sample; add your own)
  A. Building-based support team
  B. IEP
  C. Title I

III. Procedures and School Culture Protocols
  A. Fire drill and other building-exiting procedures
  B. Protocols and expectations that are not written (how teachers get lunch and where they eat)
  C. School customs for holidays or staff birthdays
  D. Sending students to the nurse (from colds to crisis—how to know the difference)
  E. Getting support for students in crisis (home problems that students bring to school)
  F. Guidelines for referring students for misbehavior (Where do they go? What do you write?)
  G. Supervisory duties and expectations for new teachers (hall duty, cafeteria?)
  H. How and where to make copies for lessons
  I. The location of books and resources needed to teach
  J. How to use the library to enhance teaching resources (school or public)

IV. Building Floor Plan and School Organization
  A. Map of school with room numbers and exits clearly labeled (nurse, office, workrooms)
  B. Map of school yard where buses drop off students, and where students enter and exit
  C. Policies for setting up classrooms

V. Teacher Union Information and State Licensing Information
  A. Representatives—meeting them
  B. Understanding paying dues
  C. Reviewing your teacher contract and state requirements

## The First Days and Weeks of School

*Organizing the classroom.*  Draw a floor plan and share it with your mentor. Can all the students see you from that teaching location? Do they need to see you? Draw out possible traffic flow as well as fire exits.

*Establishing routines.*  Discuss the important routines that need to be established on day 1. How will you share these routines with the students? Why are they important? Ask your mentor to share her or his routines for beginning the school year.

*Deciding what to do the first day of school.*  Ask for the agendas the mentors in the school have used on the first day of classes. What are appropriate first-day activities? For example, high school students need to know how to move from one classroom to the next.

*Acquiring materials for teaching in the first weeks of school.*  How and where do you get books, supplies, and materials? Ask for help so you can start the year off in an organized way.

You don't know what you don't know! *Ask* your mentor to tell you what you need to know to get started successfully!

## Other Support Systems for New Teachers: University Connections

If you have been through a teacher preparation program, you may be able to access resources that will assist you this year. Find out what is available.

1. Does your university expect to follow their graduates into the first years of teaching? If yes, how are they planning to help? Is it local or online? Do you know professors who could help you?

2. Does your university provide any support for mentor teachers? Online courses or websites? Can you take these courses? Are there any events you should be attending? Professional development workshops that would help you?

3. Is your university partnered with any universities in the area who provide support to new teachers?

4. What materials do you have from student teaching that you could use right now to get you started?

5. Are you considering a masters degree or other course work?

Ask your mentor if there are any districtwide programs for new teachers and their mentors.

# District Evaluation and Support Groups

### Evaluations

When are you evaluated? How will it be done? By the principal or by the department chair? How many observations will you have the first year? Ask your mentor to find out for you so you don't get caught off guard!

Your mentor is usually not your evaluator. Double-check to be sure that is the case in this district or school. Your mentor may assist you in preparing for the evaluation. Information about the evaluation cycle and the expectations for the new teachers in this school would be helpful. Just ask.

### Teacher Induction Support and Groups

Many districts provide special professional development sessions on hot topics such as classroom management, special needs modifications, working with English language learners, and other issues. You are encouraged to attend if they are not required. Knowledge is power for a new teacher. Time is always a factor, but this information can only help.

Use this guide as a professional development course if district induction support is not provided. Bring small groups of new teachers together with groups of experienced colleagues to promote informal sharing. Simply *sharing* ideas will provide you with practical, successful ideas and will also make you feel part of a professional group. Make time for these valuable activities.

Mentoring is only one component of effective teaching induction. Orientation and professional development are also important.

## New-Teacher Needs

What do you need this month?

How can you get support?

List some possible people who can help you.

August

## ● REFLECTions

**Directions:** Complete as many of the bubble prompts as you like after you have finished the activities in the chapter and before you set goals. Add your own prompts to blank bubbles if the prompts listed do not meet your needs. Compare and share your reflections with your mentor and other new teachers at a scheduled meeting.

I am frustrated by . . .

I need to . . .

I am excited about . . .

I am nervous about . . .

## ● SET GOALS Based on Your Needs for Next Month's Reflection and Discussion

**Directions:**

1. Review the pages in this chapter to determine what you need to revisit next month. Use these pages for possible goal ideas. Revisit any of these topics in your new-teacher support group or with your mentor.

2. Use the following to reflect on your anticipated needs. How can your mentor or other new teachers help you?

---

### Two New-Teacher Needs I Have Right Now!

1. _____

_____

_____

2. _____

_____

_____

### My Mentor Can Assist Me in Meeting These Needs

My mentor can assist me in meeting need 1 by . . . _____

_____

My mentor can assist me in meeting need 2 by . . . _____

_____

### My New-Teacher Support Group Can Assist Me

My support group can assist me in meeting need 1 by . . . _____

_____

My support group can assist me in meeting need 2 by . . . _____

_____

*A good teacher is someone who is helpful, thoughtful, smart, knows how to teach, and loves kids.* —Third-Grade Student

# Beginning the School Year Successfully

## Creating a Community of Learners in the Classroom

**New-Teacher Phase:** Nervous and Ready

*"I feel prepared to teach but I don't know what to do the first day."*

## INTASC Principles

Review INTASC Principles 2 and 5.

● **Principle 2  Child Development and Learning Theory**
The teacher understands how children learn and develop, and can provide learning opportunities that support their intellectual, social, and personal development.

● **Principle 5  Motivation and Behavior**
The teacher uses an understanding of individual and group motivation and behavior to create a learning environment that encourages positive social interaction, active engagements in learning, and self-motivation.

## Beginning the School Year Successfully
### Creating a Community of Learners in the Classroom

A wise person once said, *"Wisdom is not knowing what to do ultimately; it is knowing what to do next."* As a new teacher you will work with a mentor and perhaps a small group of new teachers in your school or district. You need to be open to building relationships with not only your students, but your colleagues as well. Some of the teachers will be informally assisting you and others may be paid to help you set up your first classroom. If you have an assigned official mentor, it is your responsibility to work to create a positive and trusting relationship. The mentor will be working to do the same. Be open to learning new ideas and ways to approach the school year. You don't have to copy everything your mentor does, but you should be open to listening and asking questions about why she or he approaches her or his school year a certain way.

Each new teacher in the school will have different needs based on their previous experiences and teacher preparation. What do you need? How can you minimize the anxiety you are feeling in September so that you can maximize student learning in your classroom this month?

You will have questions, emotional ups and downs, and lots of ideas you want to try out this month and this year. Listen to the many ways your mentors and colleagues plan for the opening of school and explore the options with them. Mentoring is not about someone *telling* you what to do; it is about *creating* opportunities where you can discover what to do in your own classroom. It is also OK to follow exactly what your mentor is doing this month. After all, you are just getting started.

Review the pages in this chapter and check the ones you want to read and use to assist you in your own learning. Don't be afraid to ask for help!

## ● Journal Entry

**Directions:** Read the cover page and the narrative for this month. How does this month's topic, the quotes, phase, and narrative overview relate to you right now? Are you comfortable with this topic? Do you need some help? How are you feeling right now?

Use your journal to record your thoughts, feelings, and questions in a free-flowing narrative. This page is for your personal reflection; it does not need to be shared as a written document. You are, however, encouraged to share excerpts with other new teachers or with your mentor as needed.

### Reflections:

*Today . . .*

Date _____

## ● PLAN Being Mentored . . . In Action!
### *Questions for Participating in a Quality Conversation*

Participating in a mentoring conversation requires you to be fully engaged. It requires listening and being open to what your mentor is sharing. This means you need to think about the questions you have and how to ask them. It does not mean you have to copy exactly what your mentor recommends, but it does mean you will reflect on the conversations and think about what makes sense for you.

Other new teachers have had these questions in September. Check the questions that you would like to discuss with your mentor or other new teachers in your school or district.

### New Teachers' Possible Questions:

_____ Who are my students and their families?

_____ How do I create a community of learners? What does that mean?

_____ Can you review how children learn at this age level?

_____ How many of my students need support in English language learning and what should I do to help them integrate socially and academically?

_____ I need some help setting up routines in my classroom that will avoid misbehavior. Can you share some successful ways for setting up a classroom in September?

_____ What are self-motivating strategies for students?

_____ What do I do if a student misbehaves?

_____ Other questions I have . . .

## ● Be Prepared
### *Your Mentor May Also Ask You Questions!*

### Mentor's Possible Questions:

_____ What is your understanding of child/adolescent development?

_____ At which level did you complete your student teaching?

_____ How confident are you in starting the year?

_____ What can I do to assist you right now that will reduce your anxiety?

## ● Monthly Organizer

### *What I Need to Do Each Month*

**Beginning the School Year Successfully:**
**Creating a Community of Learners in the Classroom**

| *Pages in this month's chapter help me to . . .* | | |
|---|---|---|
| **PLAN** | Read the title page quotes and standards | page 39 |
| | Read the narrative page | page 40 |
| | Read "Plan Your Time Wisely" | page 44 |
| | Complete the calendar with meeting dates | page 45 |
| **CONNECT** | Review connections | page 46 |
| | Connect with other new teachers | page 46 |
| **ACT** | Review the list of choices | page 47 |
| | Complete the pages you selected | pages 50–60 |
| **REFLECT** | Complete your journal entry | page 41 |
| | Fill in the bubbles | page 61 |
| **SET GOALS** | What's next for you? | page 62 |

## ● PLAN Your Time Wisely

### What Is Important to You?

As a new teacher, you will quickly discover you don't seem to have enough time to do it all! Planning your time wisely is crucial to your success in the classroom. Schedule meetings with your mentor and other new teachers early, and put the dates and times in your planning calendar. Make these meetings a priority each month.

- Meetings with your mentor or colleagues may be held before, during, or after school.

- Schedule personal quiet time for yourself to reflect and write in this guide so you can capture your feelings, ideas, and modifications for teaching each month. You can't remember everything, and writing in this guide will document your practice so you can use this as a guide during your second year of teaching.

- Schedule time to read the pages in this guidebook that relate to you. Skim the entire book so you are familiar with the topics. It is OK to skip around or read all the classroom management pages first! Use the monthly topics as a guide for group discussions with other new or experienced teachers, or with your mentor.

### Location and Time for Meetings

Use the key at the bottom of the calendar page to indicate the time of your meeting and place it on the calendar along with the time, length of meeting, and location. Select a private location for meetings with your mentor or colleagues. Make sure you select a place where you will not be interrupted. Meetings may range from five minutes to an hour! What works for you will depend on what you need and what the focus of the meeting is for that day.

What else could you include on your calendar to keep yourself organized?

- Faculty meetings
- Parent conferences
- Professional development workshops

---

### What Do I Need to Be Successful Right Now?

---

## September Calendar

| MONDAY | TUESDAY | WEDNESDAY | THURSDAY | FRIDAY |
|--------|---------|-----------|----------|--------|
|        |         |           |          |        |
|        |         |           |          |        |
|        |         |           |          |        |
|        |         |           |          |        |
|        |         |           |          |        |

September

Key: B = Before school   D = During the day (preparation time or lunchtime)   A = After school

## ● CONNECT with People, Readings, Professional Associations, Resources, and Technology

▶ *What are the resources that exist in your school and community that could assist you in beginning the school year successfully?*

**Directions:**

1. Review your journal entry and questions from the *PLAN Being Mentored . . . In Action!* page for this month.

2. How can you *connect* with people in your school or district, readings, professional associations, resources, or technology to help you? You may complete this page by yourself, with your mentor, or with a group of new teachers.

### CONNECT *with People . . .*

Who in the school building (experienced teachers, other beginning teachers, custodians, secretaries, etc.) may be able to help with September needs?

Who or what agency in the community could provide resources or support for free or low cost?

How would parents be included in September "creating a community of learners" activities?

**Names:**

### CONNECT *with Readings, Professional Associations, and Resources . . .*

What have you read or used that could assist you in creating a community of learners? You may refer to student teaching courses and readings. You may find professional development resources and books that relate to this topic in the school library.

**Titles:**

### CONNECT *with Technology . . .*

Find websites and links that will provide information about

- Creating learning communities (search by grade level)
- Child development and learning theory (search by grade level)
- Motivational strategies for students (search by grade level)
- Beginning school year activities

**Websites:**

## ● ACTIVITIES: Select Topics for Reflection and Discussion

### *What Should I Be Thinking about in September?*

This list of activities requires you to ACT either by reflecting on a topic or discussing the topic with your mentor, other experienced teachers, or other new teachers. These activities are designed to stimulate your thinking. Write in this book so you will have documentation of your thoughts and ideas for next year's planning. You do not have to complete all activities.

## Beginning the School Year Successfully: Creating a Community of Learners in the Classroom

| | FIRST STEP: Start the month with a new-teacher support group meeting! | |
|---|---|---|
| **✓** | **Check the ACTivities from the following list that are most meaningful for you to discuss.** | **Page** |
| | ACT 1    Creating a Community of Learners in Your Classroom | 50 |
| | ACT 2    Getting to Know the Students | 51 |
| | ACT 3    Creating a Classroom Profile | 52 |
| | ACT 4    Learning about Learning Styles | 53 |
| | ACT 5    Establishing Routines | 54 |
| | ACT 6    Rules, Rewards, and Consequences | 55 |
| | ACT 7    First-Month-of-School Issues | 56 |
| | ACT 8    Organizing Your First Classroom | 57 |
| | ACT 9    Classroom and Behavior Management Issues | 58 |
| | ACT 10   Looking at Student Work | 59 |
| | ACT 11   Communicating with Parents | 60 |

## ● FIRST STEP:  Host a New-Teacher Support Group Meeting

*Have snacks and water or soft drinks available. Hold the meeting in one of your classrooms so you can see teacher ideas in action. Rotate the classroom so you all have a chance to show and tell what you are doing. The host teacher could lead the meeting. Put a colorful sign on your door that says "New-Teacher Meeting. Please do not disturb." You may also want to invite other experienced teachers in the building or district who are also interested in sharing ideas. Set ground rules so everyone has a chance to talk. Use this monthly topic as a guide to keep you focused. Assign a timekeeper and set the next meeting date!*

**First:** Welcome and introduce everyone. Take some time to go around the room and quickly share your name and grade level, and one thing that is going really well!

**Then:** Review your August new-teacher REFLECTion bubbles from this guide. If you haven't completed the bubbles, do it now, then discuss what you wrote and how you can help each other.

**Next:** Review the SET GOALS page that you completed after the August orientation. How will you meet these goals?

**Begin:** Discuss one or more topics from the ACTivities pages for this month. Which topic do most of you need to discuss right now?

**Network:** Complete the CONNECTion page together.

**Acknowledge:** Recognize what you have done so far this year and, instead of focusing on what you don't know, acknowledge your successes! Remind the group to complete the REFLECTion and SET GOALS pages on their own. The last day of the month is a good time to reflect.

**Share:** End the session with compliments for each other and at least one practical idea for beginning the school year. Take time to complete the Notes page and set a date for next month's sharing group.

## *Notes*

Something I learned in the group today . . .

Something I will use in my classroom from this meeting . . .

Questions I have to . . .

    Ask my mentor . . .

    Ask other new teachers . . .

    Ask administrators . . .

Idea to share at the next meeting . . .

# Creating a Community of Learners in Your Classroom

1. Think about the ways teachers create an environment in which all students feel comfortable and respect each other. Ask your mentor how she or he includes students of other cultures in ways that empower them to be sharing members of the classroom.

2. Invite the other new teachers to share what they know about community and team building from their teacher preparation programs.

3. Think about the following approaches and see if any of these might work for you:

   - *Integrating student sharing.* Start the day or class with five minutes of student sharing time. Rationale: Students come to school with lots of issues related to their personal lives. Getting to know each other, learning how to listen, and respecting the lives of others can enhance a classroom community.

   - *Creating partnerships in the classroom.* Allow students to work together, sit together, and support each other. Rationale: Students want to talk to each other. By organizing it, new teachers can structure the sharing and use it for academic purposes. For example, when a student is absent, his or her partner can collect all the work and share what the student needs to make up.

   - *Organizing teams.* Creating learning teams to make school more engaging for students who want to interact. Teams can work on projects, create team slogans, and challenge each other in academic ways. Rotate teams periodically to include all learners. Rationale: Teamwork is more fun for some students and teaches students how to work together.

   - *Giving compliments.* Encourage students to give each other compliments at the end of the day. Rationale: Everyone likes to hear they are doing something well. Model the compliments process with your students. Positive words create caring communities.

   - *What are your ideas for creating a positive learning environment?*

# Getting to Know the Students

Listening to students, understanding their needs, and responding to their suggestions are important ways to build relationships. Many first-year teachers make the mistake of being a friend to students and then have difficulty being a teacher later in the year. Use the ideas on this page to assist you in getting to know your students. Here are some ways to learn about your students:

1. *Create an interest survey.*  Ask students to complete a short-answer survey. Here are some sample questions:

   - What do you like most about school?
   - What do you think your strengths are in the classroom?
   - How do you learn best?
   - What is your favorite subject? Why?
   - What language do you speak at home?
   - Have you ever traveled to another country?
   - What could I help you learn this year?
   - What do you wish you could do in school?
   - What is your favorite sport or hobby?
   - Do you play a musical instrument?

   Adapt questions to meet the needs of your age group. You may have to read the questions to younger children and write their answers on the board, or they can circle a set of "smiley" faces to show their opinion.

   *Short version:*  Select one or two questions and have students write the answers on the front and back of an index card. Make sure they write their names on the cards! Read the answers carefully and note the diverse needs and skills presented in this information. You may want to create a grid with names and skills to chart the whole class. Use this information to create a classroom profile.

2. *Take photographs of each student.*  Students love this, and it will help you learn their names and faces. This may be more appropriate for younger students. A whole-class photograph is fun for all age groups.

3. *Interview as many students as possible.*  Ask them to talk about their experiences in school and how they feel they learn best. You may want to audiotape these talks for future reference. Be sure to get permission from cooperating teachers, students, and parents.

4. *Interview your mentor teacher.*  Ask him or her to identify students with special needs who will require modifications in their work and any other students who should be noted.

5. *What are your ideas for getting to know your students?*

## Creating a Classroom Profile

With your mentor teacher's assistance, create a profile of the students in your classroom. If you are teaching secondary or middle school, select one of your classes to review. Find the information about the students through observing, their class record, a written survey, interviews, a class questionnaire, and talking with other teachers. The more you know about the class, the easier it is to create and maintain a positive learning environment.

List the names of the students and complete the chart by writing one or two descriptive words for each category. When complete, you will have a summary of the class you will be working with this semester. Feel free to replace these categories with those you find more useful.

| Student Name | Gender | Culture | Age | Language | Musical Ability | Artistic Ability | Athletic Ability | Learning Style | Learning Need |
|---|---|---|---|---|---|---|---|---|---|
| | | | | | | | | | |
| | | | | | | | | | |
| | | | | | | | | | |
| | | | | | | | | | |
| | | | | | | | | | |
| | | | | | | | | | |
| | | | | | | | | | |
| | | | | | | | | | |
| | | | | | | | | | |
| | | | | | | | | | |
| | | | | | | | | | |
| | | | | | | | | | |
| | | | | | | | | | |
| | | | | | | | | | |
| | | | | | | | | | |

From Pelletier, Carol Marra. *Strategies For Successful Student Teaching: A Comprehensive Guide*, 2/e. Published by Allyn and Bacon, Boston, MA. Copyright © 2004 by Pearson Education. Reprinted by permission of the publisher.

# Learning about Learning Styles

Students learn in many ways. Being able to recognize the differences will assist you in designing lessons and bringing the students together as a team. Diversity of learning styles makes the team more resourceful, yet students also need to be aware of the differences so they don't argue about their different approaches.

Check your own preferred learning styles and compare them with those of your mentor teacher. Review current learning-style theories and translate theory into practice by observing students. Many of these theorists have short learning-style tests that are available for use. Check with the school guidance counselor or adjustment counselor for details.

Ask the students how they think they learn best. Students know what they prefer and which methods work best for them. Think of ways to train students to build on their own learning strengths so they can adjust conditions to suit them. Assist students in becoming more comfortable with several learning styles.

1. Review your students' learning styles.

   ____ auditory          ____ visual          ____ hands-on          ____ random

   ____ sequential          ____ inductive          ____ deductive

   Most students are a combination of several styles, but have a preferred approach.

2. Interview several students in the classroom about their preferred learning style. Ask each student why he or she prefers this style. If a student uses a combination, list them.

   *Student*                          *Preferred Styles*                          *Reason*

   _____          _____

   _____          _____

   _____          _____

   _____          _____

   _____          _____

## Establishing Routines

Routines are important for maintaining consistency and moving through a teaching day in a manner that students can expect. Routines can save valuable time and energy that can be put into academic areas. Routines can also be used to teach respect, to model expected behaviors, and in general, to promote the positive attitude and environment you are seeking to create in the classroom.

As you observe or discuss routines with your mentor teacher, think about the following:

1.  What is the purpose of the routine?
2.  Are the students familiar with this routine? How do you know?
3.  How does your mentor teacher reinforce a routine already established?
4.  How does your mentor teacher present a new routine to the class?
5.  What other skills are students learning while participating in this routine?
6.  Are routines saving time that can be used for teaching?

### Routine Categories and Examples

I. Examples of *Opening Routines*
   A. Attendance and how to handle students who are absent so they get work
   B. Lunch count
   C. Collecting homework and recording it

II. Examples of *Operating Procedures*
   A. Walking to classes
   B. Leaving during class time
   C. Fire drills

III. Examples of *Teaching Routines*
   A. Expected behavior in classroom
   B. Class discussion procedures for listening to others
   C. Noise level for group work
   D. Students who forget books or materials
   E. What students do when they finish early

IV. Examples of *Closing Routines*
   A. Collecting work
   B. Leaving classroom
   C. Cleaning up

List other routines you observe. What have you learned about routines and their effect on the classroom learning environment?

# Rules, Rewards, and Consequences

Discuss ways rules are created in this school and in the various classrooms. How do rules, rewards, and consequences contribute to establishing a community of learners?

Work with your mentor or other new teachers to establish systems that are fair and equitable to all students.

1. What are some ground rules that are fair?

2. How will you let students know what the consequences are *prior* to them breaking a rule?

3. Ask your mentor for his or her best advice for setting up a classroom for the first time. Put your notes here.

**Date** _____

Respond to these questions today.

1. What are your problems, issues, and concerns about this topic today?

   _____

   _____

2. How are you establishing ground rules for talking in class?

   _____

   _____

3. What is working right now?

   _____

   _____

Find out how the school and district rules relate to your classroom rules.

## First-Month-of-School Issues

Ask your mentor or other teachers in the building the following questions and note what they say here.

How to . . .

- Sign out books from the resource center or library
- Use audiovisual equipment, where to get it and how to sign it out
- Reserve books for class lessons
- Get all paper and school supplies
- Deal with medical emergencies
- Access student records
- Call for a substitute and leave work for the day

Procedures . . .

- Before school, entering the building
- Homeroom protocols
- Recess and snack time
- Study hall

Space . . .

- Faculty-only rooms
- Student and faculty rooms
- Lunchrooms for faculty
- Meeting rooms
- Storage closets
- Book rooms
- Supply rooms

Using an aide or paraprofessional in the classroom

Communicating with parents

# Organizing Your First Classroom

Every new teacher has a story to tell about setting up his or her first classroom. These stories range from walking into a totally empty space to walking into a classroom that the last teacher left with 30 years of stuff piled everywhere. What's your story? The real story begins with what you are going to do with what you have been handed. Ask your mentor and school administrator for advice. There may be building codes for setting up desks or bulletin boards in certain ways. There may also be school cultural procedures that teachers have followed for years that you may be interested in knowing. Use the following topics and questions to guide you as you organize your space. Of course, you may be one of the many new teachers who does not have a space and you have to move from room to room! Get some advice now on how you will do that!

1. Desks and chairs

   *Students.*  Are they in traditional rows? Groups? Tables and chairs or desks attached? How can you set them up to maximize your ability to walk around the room and talk to individual students? Draw a picture of your ideal classroom and keep it in this book. See how it evolves throughout the year. Take a photo when you have the classroom set up for the first day of school.

   *Teachers.*  Are you the only teacher using this room or will you need to share? Are there two desks? Will paraprofessional teachers visit your classroom and require workspace? Are there any other adults who will need to visit your classroom regularly?

2. Visual Experience

   What do students see when they walk into the room? It is just the beginning of the year and you may not have anything on the walls yet, but what is your plan? Will you have a place to hang student work? Inspirational posters? Current events or news? Bulletin boards that capture the topics you are studying? You are the master of your own universe (subject to school rules, of course), so think creatively about what would entice students to enter your classroom. What color is your room? Can you change it? Ask your mentor for advice. What can you do to make this space inviting to students and other adults, as well as comfortable for you?

# Classroom and Behavior Management Issues

### Classroom Routines and Organization

1. Observe or interview how other teachers organize their space, time, and materials. Ask them to share their systems with you. What is working for them?

2. Ask your mentor or other teachers how to create systems for correcting papers, organizing materials, and grading student work.

3. Walk around the building to see how other teachers organize their space. Make notes here.

4. Ask your mentor how you take care of "housekeeping" activities required (such as collecting lunch money or homework) to minimize time spent away from classroom instruction.

### Behavior Issues with Individual Students or the Whole Class

If you are having any problems right now, speak with your mentor.

*Problem:*                                    *Suggested Solution:*

Connect with other teachers in the building who have creative ways to avoid behavioral problems in their classrooms. Discuss immediately appropriate disciplinary actions for situations that arise. Discuss the difference between students not completing homework and students who are seriously disrespectful to others.

## Looking at Student Work

Ask your mentor and other new and experienced teachers to bring samples of student work to a meeting. If they created a rubric, ask them to bring that as well. Work in pairs and have your partner randomly select three student papers (without looking at names).

1. Ask your partner what he or she notices about the completed work. Compare and contrast papers. Which students meet the objective of the assignment? How do you know? Which students did not? How do you know?

2. Rate the papers using the rubric. If you do not have a rubric, create one together. List the rubric indicators:

| 1 | 2 | 3 | 4 | 5 |
|---|---|---|---|---|
|   |   |   |   |   |
|   |   |   |   |   |
|   |   |   |   |   |

3. What is difficult about looking at student work?

4. Why is it important to look at student work?

5. How skilled are you as a new teacher in looking at student work? What is your next step to get better at this?

September

# Communicating with Parents

Read this page and review it. If you have a formally assigned mentor, discuss these and other ways you could communicate with parents in September. How can you find out which students in your class(es) are new to the district and school? It is important to welcome new students and assist them in integrating with others who have been together for years. Examples for communication may include the following:

- *A letter mailed to the home.* Ask to see samples of letters that have been sent to parents from other teachers in the school. If the school sends a formal letter welcoming students, ask for a copy. Some teachers write a letter directly to the students in their classes. Find out if this is expected.

- *A letter sent via the students.* It may be easier to write a letter and give it to the students to hand deliver to the parents sometime during the first week of school. You may want to request a return receipt to ensure the parents or guardians received the communication.

- *An email to parents.* Some school systems have parent communication through email. Find out if this is an option at your school. The downside for email is that the parents then have access to you 24 hours a day, and this may be overwhelming for you as a new teacher.

Letters to parents could include a brief biography, welcoming phrases, some examples of the curriculum you will teach this year, and ways the parents can keep in touch. Policies for homework and expectations for materials students should bring to class may also be included.

*Discuss with your mentor why it is important to connect with parents early in the year. Some examples are*

- Sets up a professional relationship before parent conferences
- Demonstrates you are  reaching out to share what is going on in the classroom
- Allows you to share expectations for learning and homework to gain parental support

Based on responses from parents, you will get an early indication of who is willing and able to connect, those parents who may not speak English, or parents who work night shifts and can't attend meetings. This gives you time to create alternate ways to communicate throughout the school year.

From Pelletier, Carol M. *Mentoring In Action: A Month-by-Month Curriculum For Mentors And Their New Teachers*, 1/e. Published by Allyn and Bacon, Boston, MA. Copyright © 2006 by Pearson Education. Reprinted by permission of the publisher.

## ● REFLECTions

**Directions:** Complete as many of the bubble prompts as you like after you have finished the activities in the chapter and before you set goals. Add your own prompts to blank bubbles if the prompts listed do not meet your needs. Compare and share your reflections with your mentor and other new teachers at a scheduled meeting.

I love . . .

I am excited about . . .

I am having difficulty with . . .

My mentor could help me . . .

## ● SET GOALS Based on Your Needs for Next Month's Reflection and Discussion

### Directions:

1. Review the pages in this chapter to determine what you need to revisit next month. Use these pages for possible goal ideas. Revisit any of these topics in your new-teacher support group or with your mentor.

2. Use the following to reflect on your anticipated needs. How can your mentor or other new teachers help you?

| Two New-Teacher Needs I Have Right Now! |
|---|
| 1. _____ |
| _____ |
| _____ |
| 2. _____ |
| _____ |
| _____ |

| My Mentor Can Assist Me in Meeting These Needs |
|---|
| My mentor can assist me in meeting need 1 by . . . _____ |
| _____ |
| My mentor can assist me in meeting need 2 by . . . _____ |
| _____ |

| My New-Teacher Support Group Can Assist Me |
|---|
| My support group can assist me in meeting need 1 by . . . _____ |
| _____ |
| My support group can assist me in meeting need 2 by . . . _____ |
| _____ |

# October

*A good teacher walks around the classroom helping everyone do things they don't understand.* —Seventh-Grade Student

# Teaching for Understanding
## Planning and Delivering Effective Instruction

### New-Teacher Phase: Overwhelmed

*"There is so much to do in one day!"*

## INTASC Principles

Review INTASC Principles 1 and 7.

- **Principle 1   Making Content Meaningful**
  The teacher understands the central concepts, tools of inquiry, and structures of the disciplines he or she teaches and creates learning experiences that make these aspects of subject matter meaningful for students.

- **Principle 7   Planning for Instruction**
  The teacher plans instruction based upon knowledge of subject matter, students, the community, and curriculum goals.

## Teaching for Understanding
### Planning and Delivering Effective Instruction

Getting through the first two months of school takes energy and lots of support. As a new teacher you need to find a safe place to talk and share what is really happening in your classroom. You may be overwhelmed by the amount of work you need to accomplish in any given day and you may be afraid to share that thought with anyone in the school. "What will they think of me?" may cross your mind. If you seek out other new teachers to talk to, you will quickly find out that you all feel the same way. Use each other for support. Write your reflections together (see the bubbles at the end of this chapter) and share your ideas. Use your mentors to help you think about how to plan and deliver effective instruction as effectively as possible, given the fact you are doing this for the first time. Be gentle with yourself!

What are your students expected to know and be able to do? How can you understand the curriculum in a way that you can teach it effectively? Many of you have never taught before, and it takes time to learn the content that needs to be taught to students, even if you passed all the state tests. Talk to other teachers about the content of the curriculum. Ask questions. Use the ACTivities pages to uncover what you already know about teaching and focus on the topics that you will find most useful this month.

What kind of expertise or life skills do you bring to the classroom? How can you use them in the classes you are teaching? Do you have computer skills? Share your current ideas and skills with your mentor and other teachers in the school. They will love it! Most teachers are lifelong learners and want to pick up new skills. Don't be shy.

New teachers have shared that there are three specific topics that they need to review every month. So you will see the topics Classroom and Behavior Management, Looking at Student Work, and Communicating with Parents in every chapter. If you have a particular need to read all the Classroom and Behavior Management topics now, do it! Then you can review the topics again each month. These discussions are ongoing throughout your professional life and will not be learned or mastered in one month.

## ● Journal Entry

**Directions:** Read the cover page and the narrative for this month. How does this month's topic, the quotes, phase, and narrative overview relate to you right now? Are you comfortable with this topic? Do you need some help? How are you feeling right now?

Use your journal to record your thoughts, feelings, and questions in a free-flowing narrative. This page is for your personal reflection; it does not need to be shared as a written document. You are, however, encouraged to share excerpts with other new teachers or with your mentor as needed.

## Reflections:

*Today . . .*

Date _____

## ● PLAN Being Mentored . . . In Action!
### *Questions for Participating in a Quality Conversation*

Participating in a mentoring conversation requires you to be fully engaged. It requires listening and being open to what your mentor is sharing. This means you need to think about the questions you have and how to ask them. It does not mean you have to copy exactly what your mentor recommends, but it does mean you will reflect on the conversations and think about what makes sense for you.

Other new teachers have had these questions in October. Check the questions that you would like to discuss with your mentor or other new teachers in your school or district.

### New Teachers' Possible Questions:

_____ What does the district expect of me as a first-year teacher?

_____ How can I learn the district curriculum and goals?

_____ How do I make content meaningful when I have the test scores as outcomes of success?

_____ How much planning do I have to do? Are my plans reviewed by the principal?

_____ Will I be observed this month?

_____ How can I "backward" plan so I can get through the content in a timely way?

_____ Can you give me some successful strategies for engaging learners in interactive ways that won't lead to misbehavior?

_____ Other questions I have . . .

## ● Be Prepared
### *Your Mentor May Also Ask You Questions!*

### Mentor's Possible Questions:

_____ What do you know about teaching for understanding? Have you taken a course that covers this topic?

_____ What do you already know about our district goals and curriculum?

_____ How do you like teachers to make content meaningful for you as a student?

_____ What can I do to assist you right now that would reduce your anxiety?

## ● Monthly Organizer

### *What I Need to Do Each Month*

**Teaching for Understanding:**
**Planning and Delivering Effective Instruction**

*October*

## ● PLAN Your Time Wisely

### What Is Important to You?

As a new teacher, you will quickly discover you don't seem to have enough time to do it all! Planning your time wisely is crucial to your success in the classroom. Schedule meetings with your mentor and other new teachers early, and put the dates and times in your planning calendar. Make these meetings a priority each month.

- Meetings with your mentor or colleagues may be held before, during, or after school.

- Schedule personal quiet time for yourself to reflect and write in this guide so you can capture your feelings, ideas, and modifications for teaching each month. You can't remember everything, and writing in this guide will document your practice so you can use this as a guide during your second year of teaching.

- Schedule time to read the pages in this guidebook that relate to you. Skim the entire book so you are familiar with the topics. It is OK to skip around or read all the classroom management pages first! Use the monthly topics as a guide for group discussions with other new or experienced teachers, or with your mentor.

### Location and Time for Meetings

Use the key at the bottom of the calendar page to indicate the time of your meeting and place it on the calendar along with the time, length of meeting, and location. Select a private location for meetings with your mentor or colleagues. Make sure you select a place where you will not be interrupted. Meetings may range from five minutes to an hour! What works for you will depend on what you need and what the focus of the meeting is for that day.

What else could you include on your calendar to keep yourself organized?

- Faculty meetings
- Parent conferences
- Professional development workshops

> ### What Do I Need to Be Successful Right Now?

# October Calendar

| MONDAY | TUESDAY | WEDNESDAY | THURSDAY | FRIDAY |
|--------|---------|-----------|----------|--------|
|  |  |  |  |  |
|  |  |  |  |  |
|  |  |  |  |  |
|  |  |  |  |  |
|  |  |  |  |  |

October

Key: B = Before school   D = During the day (preparation time or lunchtime)   A = After school

## ● CONNECT with People, Readings, Professional Associations, Resources, and Technology

▶ *What are the resources that exist in your school and community that could assist you in teaching for understanding?*

**Directions:**

1. Review your journal entry and questions from the *PLAN Being Mentored . . . In Action!* page for this month.

2. How can you *connect* with people in your school or district, readings, professional associations, resources, or technology to help you? You may complete this page by yourself, with your mentor, or with a group of new teachers.

### CONNECT *with People . . .*

Who in the school building (experienced teachers, other beginning teachers, custodians, secretaries, etc.) may be able to help with October needs?

What agencies in the community relate to the topic of "teaching for understanding"?

How can parents be helpful in helping to make content more meaningful to students?

**Names:**

### CONNECT *with Readings, Professional Associations, and Resources . . .*

What have you read or used that would assist in making content meaningful and planning effective lessons? Continue to refer to student teaching courses and readings. Ask your mentor if he or she has any books that would help.

**Titles:**

### CONNECT *with Technology . . .*

Find websites and links that will provide information about

- Teaching for understanding
- Making content meaningful at your grade level
- Lesson plans that relate to district curriculum topics
- Teaching in the content area

**Websites:**

## ● ACTIVITIES: Select Topics for Reflection and Discussion

### *What Should I Be Thinking about in October?*

This list of activities requires you to ACT by either reflecting on a topic or discussing the topic with your mentor, other experienced teachers, or other new teachers. These activities are designed to stimulate your thinking. Write in this book so you will have documentation of your thoughts and ideas for next year's planning. You do not have to complete all activities.

**October**

## Teaching for Understanding:
## Planning and Delivering Effective Instruction

| **FIRST STEP:  Start the month with a new-teacher support group meeting!** | | |
|---|---|---|
| ✓ | **Check the ACTivities from the following list that are most meaningful for you to discuss.** | **Page** |
| | ACT 1    Creating a Lesson Plan | 74 |
| | ACT 2    Planning for Understanding | 75 |
| | ACT 3    What Should the Students Know and Be Able to Do? | 76 |
| | ACT 4    Engaging Learners in Meaningful Learning Experiences | 77 |
| | ACT 5    Pacing a Lesson | 78 |
| | ACT 6    Organizing a Lesson | 79 |
| | ACT 7    Designing a Unit | 80 |
| | ACT 8    A Unit Organizer | 81 |
| | ACT 9    Classroom and Behavior Management Issues | 82 |
| | ACT 10    Looking at Student Work | 83 |
| | ACT 11    Communicating with Parents | 84 |

## ● FIRST STEP:  Host a New-Teacher Support Group Meeting

*Have snacks and water or soft drinks available. Hold the meeting in one of your classrooms so you can see teacher ideas in action. Rotate the classroom so you all have a chance to show and tell what you are doing. The host teacher could lead the meeting. Put a colorful sign on your door that says "New-Teacher Meeting. Please do not disturb." You may also want to invite other experienced teachers in the building or district who are also interested in sharing ideas. Set ground rules so everyone has a chance to talk. Use this monthly topic as a guide to keep you focused. Assign a timekeeper and set the next meeting date!*

**First:** Welcome and introduce everyone. Take some time to go around the room and quickly share your name and grade level and one thing that is going really well!

**Then:** Review your September new-teacher REFLECTions bubbles from this guide. If you haven't completed the bubbles, do it now, then discuss what you wrote and how you can help each other.

**Next:** Review the SET GOALS page that you completed after the September support group meeting. How will you meet these goals?

**Begin:** Discuss one or more topics from the ACTivities pages for this month. Which topic do most of you need to discuss right now?

**Network:** Complete the CONNECTion page together.

**Acknowledge:** Recognize what you have done so far this year and, instead of focusing on what you don't know, acknowledge your successes! Remind the group to complete the REFLECTion and SET GOALS pages on their own. The last day of the month is a good time to reflect.

**Share:** End the session with compliments for each other and at least one practical idea for beginning the school year. Take time to complete the Notes page and set a date for next month's sharing group.

## *Notes*

Something I learned in the group today . . .

Something I will use in my classroom from this meeting . . .

Questions I have to . . .

    Ask my mentor . . .

    Ask other new teachers . . .

    Ask administrators . . .

Idea to share at the next meeting . . .

October

## Creating a Lesson Plan

Discuss the following questions with your mentor. Ask him or her to share copies of his or her lesson plans.

- *Why am I teaching this lesson?* Required curriculum? Student interest? New-teacher interest? Other?

- *What do I hope to accomplish?* Skill development? Concept to be discussed for understanding? Product to be produced?

- *Who are the students?* Range of abilities? Range of ages? Ethnic diversity and varying cultures?

- *What is the time frame for teaching this lesson?* Part of a unit? One period or block schedule? Isolated lesson?

- *How will I begin the lesson to capture student attention?* Story or anecdote? Relevance to their lives? Props or visual displays?

- *Will I need other resources to teach this lesson?* Audiovisual or technology? Student handouts? Manipulatives or visual displays?

- *How will students spend their time during the lesson?* Small-group discussion? Individual? Large group? Hands-on activity or experiment? Taking notes or observing?

- *How will this lesson be assessed?* Formally? Quiz or test? Informally? Observation of learning? Open-ended questions? Written? Verbal?

- *How will I close the lesson and close the class period?* Review and summary? Collect papers? Give next assignment? Allow time for homework or questions?

- *Will there be homework or enrichment activities offered?* How will I collect them later? Is it required or extra? Will it count? What is cooperating teacher's policy? How will I grade it?

- *How will I know whether I succeeded in teaching the lesson?* Self-assessment? Response of students? Cooperating teacher input?

- *How will the next lesson relate to or build on this one?*

# Planning for Understanding

A teacher knows he or she has a good plan when, at the end of the lesson or unit, there is evidence of student understanding or skill development. An effective teacher, like an architect, designs a plan that will create a solid foundation for creative and original thinking. Teachers present information not just to be memorized for the weekly test, but to be understood and integrated into a student's thinking. This is not an easy task, but one that should be kept in your awareness as you begin to plan lessons.

What do you want students to know, understand, and be able to do *as a result of your lesson?*

### Four Steps to Meaningful Lesson Planning

1.  *Think about breadth or depth* as you design your lessons and units.

    Are you aiming for breadth in your lessons (e.g., being able to connect this concept to other concepts or relevant experiences)?
    *   Students explain why or why not.
    *   Students extend the concept to others.
    *   Students think about and give examples of similar concepts.

    Are you aiming for depth in your lessons (i.e., looking more at the details of this idea)?
    *   Students question the information.
    *   Students analyze the facts.
    *   Students prove something.

2.  *Set priorities* for assessing student growth in lessons and units.

    What do you expect all students to be familiar with?
    *   To be able to do in this class?
    *   To understand completely for lasting learning?

3.  *Select measurement tools* to determine student understanding.

    How will you know students understand?
    *   What do *all* students have to know? How will you know?
    *   What do *most* students have to know? How will you know?
    *   What will *some* students have to know? How will you know?

4.  *Create meaningful learning experiences* that engage and support learning (not just busywork).
    *   MOTIVATE—Have you included a "hook" to gain attention and provide relevance?
    *   QUESTIONS—Do you have key questions that promote discussion and thinking?
    *   PRACTICE—Do you have time for students to practice and engage in activity?
    *   SELF-ASSESSMENT—Do you allow students time to reflect on their work and set goals?

From Pelletier, Carol Marra. *Strategies For Successful Student Teaching: A Comprehensive Guide*, 2/e. Published by Allyn and Bacon, Boston, MA. Copyright © 2004 by Pearson Education. Reprinted by permission of the publisher.

## What Should the Students Know and Be Able to Do?

Objectives state what the teacher wants the students to accomplish on completion of the lesson. Students should be clear about objectives before they begin the lesson so they know what is expected of them. Objectives should be written as one sentence.

Use verbs to write your lesson plan objectives. *Bloom's Taxonomy* organizes the verbs by levels of understanding, beginning with basic knowledge and moving up through comprehension, application, analysis, synthesis, and evaluation. Higher level thinking is expected for verbs at levels 5 and 6. These verbs indicate what the student should be doing.

As you write your lesson plan objectives, select a verb and complete the sentence to state what is to be accomplished. State the objective in clear terms that can be easily understood by students and parents. Be sure to vary the levels of complexity in your lessons.

*Examples:*   Name the planets, in order from the sun.

Predict the ending to this story.

Explain the reasons for the start of the Civil War.

| Level of Understanding | Example Verbs |
|---|---|
| 6  Evaluation | choose, conclude, evaluate, defend, rank, support, rate |
| 5  Synthesis | construct, create, formulate, revise, write, plan, predict |
| 4  Analysis | analyze, classify, compare, contrast, debate, categorize |
| 3  Application | apply, demonstrate, draw, show, solve, illustrate |
| 2  Comprehension | describe, explain, paraphrase, summarize, rewrite |
| 1  Knowledge | define, identify, label, list, memorize, spell, name |

What do you, in the role of the teacher, need to do to have students experience a variety of learning objectives at all levels? *Remember, an effective teacher teaches so students meet the objectives stated in the lesson plan.*

# Engaging Learners in Meaningful Learning Experiences

How do effective teachers initially gain students' attention to shift from non-instructional announcements to instructional curriculum? Do they use a story? A prop? A question? Do they connect what is coming up in the lesson to the students' own experiences?

List ways teachers motivate and gain students' attention:

_____

_____

### The Lesson

How do effective teachers maintain this attention if there is a whole class? If there are small groups, is it different? How do they ensure all students are engaged in a learning experience? Do they walk around? How do they interact with students to keep them on task? Do they call on students?

List any "maintaining" management strategies you have observed:

_____

_____

### Closing the Lesson/Ending the Class Period

How do effective teachers complete the lesson? How do they know the students learned? How do they check for understanding? Are there noninstructional directions that need to be given at the end of class? Is there time for questions and answers, or does the lesson just end? Is there time for students to do homework? How do the teachers close the lesson and end the class period? How are these things different?

List the management techniques for closing you have observed:

_____

_____

How does opening, maintaining, and closing a lesson in a predictable and organized way contribute to student learning?

_____

_____

October

## Pacing a Lesson

One of the biggest concerns teachers have about teaching is that they don't have enough time in the day to do all there is to do. The majority of the time spent in class should be on teaching the curriculum that you have planned, not on making announcements, collecting lunch money, passing out materials, getting students into groups, or cleaning up. However, these tasks do need to get done.

A class period is your *allocated teaching time,* but it also needs to include house-keeping activities. *Instructional time* is the time when students are actually engaged in learning activities. Your lesson plan is the way to organize your thinking so that most of the allocated time is spent engaging students in learning and checking for understanding.

| Allocated Class Time: How Much Should You Spend? | | |
|---|---|---|
| How much time? | Starting class period Housekeeping activities | • Required tasks<br>• Collection of homework |
| Time: | BEGINNING LESSON Introducing or connecting to previous day | • Motivation/relevance<br>• Overview<br>• Directions<br>• Purpose of lesson |
| Time: | MIDDLE | • Objective<br>• Key questions<br>• Students engaged in learning<br>• Activity<br>• Knowledge<br>• Student sharing<br>• Informal assessment and checking for understanding |
| Time: | CLOSING | • Wrap-up<br>• Review of key points<br>• Collection of materials/papers |
| Time: | Ending class period Housekeeping activities | • Required tasks<br>• Collection of classwork |

Use the previous table as a guide and include time as a factor in designing your lesson plans. When you have a particularly complicated lesson with many materials, or if you need to move students into groups, take that into consideration during your planning and think of ways to prepare and set up so you don't take away from teaching time.

# Organizing a Lesson

**Lesson plan title:** Write the name of the topic or class here.    **Date:** Day you teach the lesson

**Time of class:** Period or time    **Length of period:** How much time to teach

**Subject:** Content

**Purpose of lesson:** Why are you teaching this lesson? What goal are you seeking to reach?

**Objective:** Bloom's taxonomy verb—what the students will achieve or accomplish

**Theme or unit no. ___:** Is this an isolated lesson or part of a bigger curriculum unit? Number it according to where it fits in the sequence. If there is an expectation that students need prior knowledge to complete the lesson, how will you handle this with new students or those who have missed previous lessons?

**Key questions:** The questions you will introduce to the students to guide the discussion and activities of the lesson should be broadly designed to encourage discussion and critical thinking. (Questions should not be designed to elicit a yes or no answer.)

**Procedure:** Note that the class period includes other housekeeping activities, such as collecting papers from the night before, announcing future school activities, or collecting lunch money. These need to be incorporated into the lesson plan to avoid running out of teaching time.

| | | | |
|---|---|---|---|
| **Sample Procedure for Use of Allotted Classroom Time** | | | |
| **Time** | **Classroom Lesson** | **Teacher Behaviors: What Will You Be Doing?** | **Expected Student Behaviors: What Will the Students Be Doing?** |
| 5% | Starting class period | Housekeeping | Listening, passing in homework |
| 10% | Beginning lesson | Introducing objectives, vocabulary, and key questions | Showing interest, participating, listening |
| 70% | Middle of lesson | Facilitating a variety of activities for student learning | Collaborating, thinking, discussing, responding to key questions |
| 10% | Closing lesson | Summarizing and reviewing lesson, and setting goals for next lesson | Answering key questions Self-assessing |
| 5% | Ending class period | Housekeeping | Passing in materials |

From Pelletier, Carol Marra. *Strategies For Successful Student Teaching: A Comprehensive Guide*, 2/e. Published by Allyn and Bacon, Boston, MA. Copyright © 2004 by Pearson Education. Reprinted by permission of the publisher.

October

# Designing a Unit

A unit is an organized group of lesson plans with a beginning, various activities, and a culmination. The unit may be subject based, interdisciplinary, or thematic. It can last as long as a semester or as short as a week. It has overarching themes and concepts to be learned through daily lessons. Teachers typically organize their teaching in units by skills for early childhood, by subjects or themes for elementary/middle school, or by subject area at secondary levels. Units are organized around books students have read, historical events, science themes, topics, or anything teachers can think of that relates to knowledge.

A unit will have a general outline or plan for implementation and the daily lesson plans that demonstrate in detail how the plan is to be carried out in the classroom. Lesson plans are created as you move through the unit, not ahead of time, because the original plan often changes.

### Questions to Consider before Beginning a Unit

- What is the purpose of the unit?
- How much time will the unit need? How many lessons?
- What do students already know?
- What would students like to learn or know?
- How will the unit be introduced?
- What are the key questions that need to be answered?
- Is prior knowledge necessary?
- Will the unit have a theme?
- Will the unit cross disciplines? Is team teaching involved?
- Will any special activities be part of the unit?
- Will I need special materials or audiovisuals for this unit?
- Will guest speakers or field trips be part of the unit?
- Other?

From Pelletier, Carol Marra. *Strategies For Successful Student Teaching: A Comprehensive Guide,* 2/e. Published by Allyn and Bacon, Boston, MA. Copyright © 2004 by Pearson Education. Reprinted by permission of the publisher.

## A Unit Organizer

An example of a unit organizer follows:

| Title of Unit | | | | |
|---|---|---|---|---|
| Purpose | Objectives | Key Questions | Key Vocabulary | Materials |
| Assessments | Possible Daily Lesson Activities | Opening Activity | Culmination | Guests or Trips |

From Pelletier, Carol Marra. *Strategies For Successful Student Teaching: A Comprehensive Guide*, 2/e. Published by Allyn and Bacon, Boston, MA. Copyright © 2004 by Pearson Education. Reprinted by permission of the publisher.

# Classroom and Behavior Management Issues

Before disciplining a student, ask your new teachers to ask themselves the following:

1. Who is the student?
   - Does this student have a prearranged plan when disruptive? For example, sent to guidance office, principal, or resource or learning center classroom?
   - Is this a first offense or is this repeated misbehavior?
   - Does this student have a special need that has not been addressed?
   - Are there other adults who need to be notified when this student is disruptive?

2. What rule did the student break?
   - Is it a major offense? For example, hitting someone or possessing a weapon.
   - Is it a minor offense? For example, chewing gum or wearing a hat.
   - Is it related to academic work? For example, not doing homework or cheating.
   - Is it related to work habits? For example, not listening in class.

3. What did the student specifically do or say?

4. Is this misbehavior appropriate for the student's age?

5. Where did the misbehavior take place?
   - In the classroom?
   - On the playground, hallway, cafeteria, en route to class?
   - Off school grounds, but near school?

6. Is this behavior a common occurrence?
   - For this student?
   - For others in the school?

7. Do you have personal feelings about this student?
   - Have you interacted positively or negatively before this?
   - Do you know this student at all?

8. What are your legal rights when dealing with disruptive students?
   - State and local guidelines for restraining students, searching lockers, and so forth?
   - School policies related to alcohol, drugs, weapons?
   - Students with educational plans?

**Notes:**

# Looking at Student Work

Ask your mentor or other new teachers to bring several samples of student work to a meeting. Review the work together and complete the following questions.

**Standards:**

What was the objective of this work?

What was the student supposed to accomplish?

**Quality:**

What did the work look like?

Was the student proud of this work?

**Expectations:**

What did you expect the student to do on this assignment?

Are your expectations limiting the student's achievement?

Discuss the importance of looking at student work systematically.

## Communicating with Parents

### Letting Parents Know What You Are Teaching

Discuss possible ways you can let the parents know about the curriculum and the routines of your classroom. Parents often ask their children, "What did you do in school today?" Students respond, "Nothing!" We all know this is not true. As a new teacher, you can be proactive in communicating with the parents of your students. Often, communication comes when there is a problem, and then parents are on the defensive. Find out the most positive ways to connect with parents in your school and try them.

### *Newsletters*

Why not put the students to work and have them write short articles about the lessons they are learning in school and turn it into a newsletter for parents? You can use this as a learning experience for students while informing parents. *Education Matters!* could be the name of the newsletter or students could vote on a name. Students can hand deliver the newsletter or it could be mailed directly to the parents.

### *Classroom Open House*

Another way you can connect with parents and share what is going on in the classroom is to host an open house in the classroom. Invite the parents in for "coffee and conversation" early in the morning before students arrive or include students. Share the logistics of this type of event with your mentor. Brainstorm ways students can show off their work and how you can let parents know how they can help their children progress.

### *Classroom Web Page*

Many teachers entering the profession have technology skills and are able to create web pages. If your school and district have the capabilities for a web-based newsletter, you may want to try this. It is a fun and easy way to get parents' attention!

### *Cable TV Show*

Another option for sharing what is going on could be a classroom TV show. Let students produce and direct a show that lets parents know what they are learning! You may not have time to create your own show, but perhaps several new teachers could get together and put on short segments. It would also be a great way to introduce yourself to the school district!

## ● REFLECTions

**Directions:** Complete as many of the bubble prompts as you like after you have finished the activites in the chapter and before you set goals. Add your own prompts to blank bubbles if the prompts listed do not meet your needs. Compare and share your reflections with your mentor and other new teachers at a scheduled meeting.

My students . . .

The parents . . .

The principal . . .

My family . . .

October

## ● SET GOALS Based on Your Needs for Next Month's Reflection and Discussion

**Directions:**

1. Review the pages in this chapter to determine what you need to revisit next month. Use these pages for possible goal ideas. Revisit any of these topics in your new-teacher support group or with your mentor.

2. Use the following to reflect on your anticipated needs. How can your mentor or other new teachers help you?

| Two New-Teacher Needs I Have Right Now! |
|---|
| 1. _____ <br> _____ <br> _____ <br><br> 2. _____ <br> _____ <br> _____ |

| My Mentor Can Assist Me in Meeting These Needs |
|---|
| My mentor can assist me in meeting need 1 by . . . _____ <br> _____ <br><br> My mentor can assist me in meeting need 2 by . . . _____ <br> _____ |

| My New-Teacher Support Group Can Assist Me |
|---|
| My support group can assist me in meeting need 1 by . . . _____ <br> _____ <br><br> My support group can assist me in meeting need 2 by . . . _____ <br> _____ |

# November

*I know I have learned something when I have the confidence to do it alone.* —Fourth-Grade Student

# Assessing Diverse Learners

## How Do Teachers Know Students Have Learned?

**New-Teacher Phase:** Disillusioned

*"I'm not sure if I made the right choice to teach. This is really hard."*

## INTASC Principles

Review INTASC Principles 3 and 8.

● **Principle 3  Learning Styles/Diversity**
The teacher understands how students differ in their approaches to learning and creates instructional opportunities that are adapted to diverse learners.

● **Principle 8  Assessment**
The teacher understands and uses formal and informal assessment strategies to evaluate and ensure the continuous intellectual, social, and physical development of the learner.

## Assessing Diverse Learners

### How Do Teachers Know Students Have Learned?

Confidence and competence are important feelings for a new teacher and you may not feel either right now. In November, you may feel overwhelmed and disillusioned, wondering why and how you got into this career. Turn to your mentor and other new teachers for support. This is a normal phase of teaching! We all went through it the first year. In fact, many veteran teachers are disillusioned in November.

Review the fourth grade student's quote on the first page of this chapter, "I know I have learned something when I have the confidence to do it alone." In some ways, this is you. As you become comfortable with the content you are required to teach, you gain more confidence in yourself as a teacher. You are a learner this year, just like your own students. Ask yourself how much your students are learning so far this year. Then ask yourself how much you are learning about how to teach students how to learn.

Use the ACTivities in this chapter to discuss important ways to tap into students' prior knowledge and monitor their progress. Ask your mentor how he or she does this. Learning styles of students will affect the assessments you use to measure growth. What is your role as a teacher in learning how to assess diverse learners? Remember, you have your own learning style and teaching style.

Review all the pages for November to see what your focus will be. Write in them. Put notes on them. Add stickers! Highlight key phrases. This is your journey. You will want to have this document to review next year.

## ● Journal Entry

**Directions:** Read the cover page and the narrative for this month. How does this month's topic, the quotes, phase, and narrative overview relate to you right now? Are you comfortable with this topic? Do you need some help? How are you feeling right now?

Use your journal to record your thoughts, feelings, and questions in a free-flowing narrative. This page is for your personal reflection; it does not need to be shared as a written document. You are, however, encouraged to share excerpts with other new teachers or with your mentor as needed.

### Reflections:

*Today . . .*

Date _____

## ● PLAN Being Mentored . . . In Action!

### *Questions for Participating in a Quality Conversation*

Participating in a mentoring conversation requires you to be fully engaged. It requires listening and being open to what your mentor is sharing. This means you need to think about the questions you have and how to ask them. It does not mean you have to copy exactly what your mentor recommends, but it does mean you will reflect on the conversations and think about what makes sense for you.

Other new teachers have had these questions in November. Check the questions that you would like to discuss with your mentor or other new teachers in your school or district.

#### New Teachers' Possible Questions:

_____ Who are my students (languages, learning styles, special needs, learning modifications, family background, etc.)?

_____ What do I need to know about their parents that will assist me?

_____ How can I set up my lessons and learning to adapt for the needs of my diverse learners?

_____ What high-stakes formal assessments are part of district expectations?

_____ What formal assessments should I be creating or using this year?

_____ Can you review informal assessment with me and share when you think I should be doing it?

_____ Other questions I have . . .

## ● Be Prepared

### *Your Mentor May Also Ask You Questions!*

#### Mentor's Possible Questions:

_____ What do you already know about tests and assessment?

_____ What do you already know about teaching diverse learners?

_____ Share one strategy you have used that assisted a student who was struggling to learn new information.

_____ What can I do to assist you right now that would reduce your anxiety?

## ● Monthly Organizer
### *What I Need to Do Each Month*

**Assessing Diverse Learners**
**How Do Teachers Know Students Have Learned?**

| *Pages in this month's chapter help me to . . .* | | |
|---|---|---|
| **PLAN** | Read the title page quotes and standards | page 87 |
| | Read the narrative page | page 88 |
| | Read "Plan Your Time Wisely" | page 92 |
| | Complete the calendar with meeting dates | page 93 |
| **CONNECT** | Review connections | page 94 |
| | Connect with other new teachers | page 94 |
| **ACT** | Review the list of choices | page 95 |
| | Complete the pages you selected | pages 98–110 |
| **REFLECT** | Complete your journal entry | page 89 |
| | Fill in the bubbles | page 111 |
| **SET GOALS** | What's next for you? | page 112 |

November

## ● PLAN Your Time Wisely

### *What Is Important to You?*

As a new teacher, you will quickly discover you don't seem to have enough time to do it all! Planning your time wisely is crucial to your success in the classroom. Schedule meetings with your mentor and other new teachers early, and put the dates and times in your planning calendar. Make these meetings a priority each month.

- Meetings with your mentor or colleagues may be held before, during, or after school.

- Schedule personal quiet time for yourself to reflect and write in this guide so you can capture your feelings, ideas, and modifications for teaching each month. You can't remember everything, and writing in this guide will document your practice so you can use this as a guide during your second year of teaching.

- Schedule time to read the pages in this guidebook that relate to you. Skim the entire book so you are familiar with the topics. It is OK to skip around or read all the classroom management pages first! Use the monthly topics as a guide for group discussions with other new or experienced teachers, or with your mentor.

### *Location and Time for Meetings*

Use the key at the bottom of the calendar page to indicate the time of your meeting and place it on the calendar along with the time, length of meeting, and location. Select a private location for meetings with your mentor or colleagues. Make sure you select a place where you will not be interrupted. Meetings may range from five minutes to an hour! What works for you will depend on what you need and what the focus of the meeting is for that day.

What else could you include on your calendar to keep yourself organized?

- Faculty meetings
- Parent conferences
- Professional development workshops

---

*What Do I Need to Be Successful Right Now?*

---

The First Year Matters: Being Mentored . . . In Action!

## November Calendar

| MONDAY | TUESDAY | WEDNESDAY | THURSDAY | FRIDAY |
|--------|---------|-----------|----------|--------|
| | | | | |
| | | | | |
| | | | | |
| | | | | |
| | | | | |

November

Key: B = Before school  D = During the day (preparation time or lunchtime)  A = After school

## ● CONNECT with People, Readings, Professional Associations, Resources, and Technology

▶ *What are the resources that exist in your school and community that could assist you in assessing diverse learners?*

**Directions:**

1. Review your journal entry and questions from the PLAN Being Mentored . . . In Action! page for this month.

2. How can you *connect* with people in your school or district, readings, professional associations, resources, or technology to help you? You may complete this page by yourself, with your mentor, or with a group of new teachers.

### CONNECT *with People . . .*

Who in the school building (experienced teachers, other beginning teachers, custodians, secretaries, etc.) may be able to help with November needs?

What agencies in the community relate to the topic of assessing diverse learners?

How can parents help in having new teachers understand students' learning styles?

**Names:**

### CONNECT *with Readings, Professional Associations, and Resources . . .*

What have you read or used that would assist in the areas of diversity, assessment, and learning styles? You may refer to student teaching courses and readings. Your mentor may have books that relate to these topics.

**Titles:**

### CONNECT *with Technology . . .*

Find websites and links that will provide information about

- Learning styles and teaching styles
- Diverse learners
- Informal assessment strategies (search by grade levels and disciplines)
- Formal assessments
- High-stakes tests for your state and district
- No Child Left Behind Act

**Websites:**

## ● ACTIVITIES: Select Topics for Reflection and Discussion

### What Should I Be Thinking about in November?

This list of activities requires you to ACT by either reflecting on a topic or discussing the topic with your mentor, other experienced teachers, or other new teachers. These activities are designed to stimulate your thinking. Write in this book so you will have a documentation of your thoughts and ideas for next year's planning. You do not have to complete all activities.

November

### Assessing Diverse Learners:
### How Do Teachers Know Students Have Learned?

| FIRST STEP: Start the month with a new-teacher support group meeting! | | |
|---|---|---|
| ✓ | **Check the ACTivities from the following list that are most meaningful for you to discuss.** | **Page** |
| | ACT 1    How Are Students Assessed and Evaluated? | 98 |
| | ACT 2    Linking Lesson Plans to Assessment | 99 |
| | ACT 3    Tapping in to Students' Prior Knowledge | 100 |
| | ACT 4    A Variety of Ways to Observe Student Learning | 101 |
| | ACT 5    Formative and Summative Assessments | 102 |
| | ACT 6    Using Rubrics and Portfolios to Assess Performance | 103 |
| | ACT 7    Documenting Progress and Record-Keeping Strategies | 104 |
| | ACT 8    Can Students Monitor Their Own Progress? | 105 |
| | ACT 9    Communicating with Students about Their Progress | 106 |
| | ACT 10   Classroom and Behavior Management Issues | 107 |
| | ACT 11   Looking at Student Work | 108 |
| | ACT 12   Communicating with Parents | 109 |
| | ACT 13   New-Teacher Needs | 110 |

## ● FIRST STEP: Host a New-Teacher Support Group Meeting

*Have snacks and water or soft drinks available. Hold the meeting in one of your classrooms so you can see teacher ideas in action. Rotate the classroom so you all have a chance to show and tell what you are doing. The host teacher could lead the meeting. Put a colorful sign on your door that says "New-Teacher Meeting. Please do not disturb." You may also want to invite other experienced teachers in the building or district who are also interested in sharing ideas. Set ground rules so everyone has a chance to talk. Use this monthly topic as a guide to keep you focused. Assign a timekeeper and set the next meeting date!*

**First:** Welcome and introduce everyone. Take some time to go around the room and quickly share your name and grade level and one thing that is going really well!

**Then:** Review your October new-teacher REFLECTions bubbles from this guide. If you haven't completed the bubbles, do it now, then discuss what you wrote and how you can help each other.

**Next:** Review the SET GOALS page that you completed after the October support group meeting. How will you meet these goals?

**Begin:** Discuss one or more topic from the ACTivities pages for this month. Which topic do most of you need to discuss right now?

**Network:** Complete the CONNECTions page together.

**Acknowledge:** Recognize what you have done so far this year and instead of focusing on what you don't know, acknowledge your successes! Remind the group to complete the REFLECTions and SET GOALS pages on their own. The last day of the month is a good time to reflect.

**Share:** End the session with compliments for each other and at least one practical idea for November. Take time to complete the Notes page and set a date for next month's sharing group.

## *Notes*

Something I learned in the group today . . .

Something I will use in my classroom from this meeting . . .

Questions I have to . . .

    Ask my mentor . . .

    Ask other new teachers . . .

    Ask administrators . . .

Idea to share at the next meeting . . .

November

## How Are Students Assessed and Evaluated?

Ask your mentor what types of tests the students will take this year. Review the purposes of the tests and find out the procedures. Learn about state and local tests and how they relate to the environment for learning you are attempting to create with your students.

### State Testing Initiatives

Does the state have a statewide testing program? What is its purpose?

Are the students required to pass a high school exit exam? When is it given? What is the test? Are there other state tests required? Which grade levels? Ask to review a copy of the tests if they are at your grade level.

On what standards or frameworks are the tests based? How will this state test affect the curriculum you teach in your classroom?

### District Testing Program

What is the purpose of these tests?

Does the district require tests for certain grades? Note the test names here.

Are these tests similar to the state tests? How?

### Classroom Assessment and Evaluation Procedures

How will you use *informal assessment* to assess learning? Journals? Note cards? File folders? Portfolios? Notes in rank book? Ask your mentor about his or her strategies.

How will you *formally assess* students for understanding? Teacher-made tests? Publishing company tests? Performance assessment? Portfolios? Find out which assessment tools this grade level is using.

## Linking Lesson Plans to Assessment

Lesson planning and assessment are linked. Remember that the lesson plan and assessment or evaluation of the lesson should be written at the same time. This ensures that students will be responding to the key questions and objectives established for learning. What do you want students to be able to do? What will students know as a result of this lesson?

Ask your mentor to share a lesson plan she recently created. Were the objectives clear? Did she know what she wanted students to learn? What type of assessment did she create? Did her assessment approach match your lesson's activities?

How do other teachers create forms of assessment in this school? Talk with other teachers about assessment. They can share at your next new-teacher support meeting.

November

## Tapping in to Students' Prior Knowledge

An important aspect of assessment is knowing where students are before you begin teaching. Students come to the classroom with varied backgrounds and experience levels related to the topic you may be presenting. Being able to assess this knowledge as part of your regular planning process is important to designing lessons that meet the needs of the diverse learners in your classroom. English language learners need support.

1. Find out how experienced teachers have tapped in to students' prior knowledge.

2. How have you observed other teachers tapping in to students' prior knowledge?

Ways to tap in . . .

1. Ask students privately on paper before the lesson begins . . .
   - What do you already know about this topic/skill?
   - What do you think you know or have you heard about this topic/skill?
   - What would you like to learn or know?
2. Collect the papers. At the end of the unit or lesson, ask what they learned and have them write it on the bottom of the sheet they had previously started.
3. Give a pretest on the topic, testing for spelling words, math skill, and so on.
4. Have students write a paragraph about what they know about the topic.

Tapping in can avoid teaching students who may already *know* the information. It also assists you in designing lessons to meet the current needs of your students. Tapping in can also serve as a check-in toward the middle and near the end of the term to let you know how closely the lesson objectives are being met.

# A Variety of Ways to Observe Student Learning

How do you observe student achievement? Will a product let you know that the student achieved the objectives or do you need to observe the student perform and demonstrate the skill or understanding of the topic? Learn the difference between *product* and *process* assessment. Note that the assessment/evaluation depends on the lesson's objective. Be sure the achievement measure matches the objective designed in your lesson plan. Suggestions for product and process assessments include the following:

| Product (Paper/Pencil) | Product (Visual) | Performance Process (with or without Product) |
| --- | --- | --- |
| Essays | Posters | Oral reports |
| Book reports | Banners | Speeches |
| Biographies | Models | Raps |
| Journals | Diagrams | Dramatizations |
| Letters | Displays | Debates |
| Editorials | Videotapes or audiotapes | Songs |
| Scripts | Portfolios | Poems |
| Tests | Exhibits | Demonstrations |
| Research reports | Paintings | Interviews |
| Short answers | Photos | Skits |
| Position papers | Websites | News reports |

Look at your lessons. Do they always require the same type of assessment or evaluation? Are you providing alternative assessments for all learners?

November

# Formative and Summative Assessments

### Formative Assessment Is Practice—The Dress Rehearsal

It is authentic, ongoing, sit beside, self-assessing, learn as we go, practice, group work, conversations, checklists, surveys, drills, practice tests. When will you use formative assessments in teaching?

### Summative Assessment Is Final—The Opening Night of the Play

It is the final test, grade given to an individual student, final evaluation, judgment made at the end of the unit or term, report card grade, SAT final score, paper test, project artwork, final performance, oral exam. When will you use summative evaluation?

From Pelletier, Carol Marra. *Strategies For Successful Student Teaching: A Comprehensive Guide*, 2/e. Published by Allyn and Bacon, Boston, MA. Copyright © 2004 by Pearson Education. Reprinted by permission of the publisher.

# Using Rubrics and Portfolios to Assess Performance

Rubrics are either holistic or analytical. Holistic scoring values the student's overall thinking and understanding. The score is applied to the overall quality of the task completed. Analytical rubrics award points for each step the student completes in the process. Review samples of rubrics with your mentor or new-teacher support group.

1. Discuss specific criteria for a good paper, project, or performance.

2. Define degrees of understanding and demonstration. Examples include the following:
   - *Accuracy:* Completely accurate, almost accurate, not accurate
   - *Clarity:* Thoughts are clear, thoughts are hard to understand
   - *Understanding:* Complete, almost, doesn't understand

3. Discuss student portfolios. Share samples and ask other new teachers or mentors to explain what they know about this topic.

*November*

# Documenting Progress and Record-Keeping Strategies

Teachers use a variety of systems to keep track of student progress. A common way is to use a gradebook. However, many teachers use different systems within their gradebooks. Ask your mentor to share his or her system with you. What does his or her system include?

In addition to using gradebooks, you may make anecdotal comments and use journals, index file boxes, or make notes in your planning book to keep track. Other teachers use checklists or progress charts. Find three other ways to record information and indicate why a teacher might use these systems in addition to a gradebook.

1. _____

2. _____

3. _____

How do you decide whether a record-keeping system is effective? Ask yourself . . .

- Is it easy to use? (Is it something I will use?)
- Is it easy to read? (Can you scan it quickly for information?)
- Can I derive patterns from it? (Over time, do I see student progress?)

**Two Tips**

1. Use a highlighter to mark the "holes" in your gradebook to scan for missing grades easily.
2. Use another color highlighter to mark any grade below average to scan problem areas quickly.

From Pelletier, Carol Marra. *Strategies For Successful Student Teaching: A Comprehensive Guide*, 2/e. Published by Allyn and Bacon, Boston, MA. Copyright © 2004 by Pearson Education. Reprinted by permission of the publisher.

# Can Students Monitor Their Own Progress?

### Hard or Easy?
- Ask students whether they are finding the work hard or easy.
- Make a graph to see how many students are finding things hard or easy.

### What Are You Learning?
- Take a minute at the end of each class as part of your closing to ask students to write two things they learned in class today.
- Collect and review their papers to see how you did as a teacher in presenting your objectives. This exercise can serve two purposes: (1) to see what they recall and (2) to let you know how to plan the next lesson.

### More Time?
- Have students vote whether they think they need more time on a concept.
- Let students reply anonymously on paper or by putting their heads down and raising their hands.
- Write your own prediction of how the lesson went and what they will say before reading the students' responses.

### Work Habits
Create a worksheet that includes statements that the students have to rate from one to five. For example:
- I worked hard in groups today.
- I understand the concepts presented.

### Teacher Assessment
Create a worksheet for your students about you and your skills in teaching. Have them rate each factor on a scale from one to five. For example:
- My teacher presents information in a way I can understand.
- My teacher listens to my questions.
- There is time in class for me to practice the skills that are being taught.

November

# Communicating with Students about Their Progress

Teachers use a variety of systems to communicate with their students and to keep them on track. The most common formats are the *progress slip* and the *report card.* Many teachers show these to students first, before they are sent home. Remember that progress may include growth in behavior as well as academics.

In addition to these traditional approaches, teachers are using other procedures to communicate directly with students. Discuss and share samples/ideas of any of the following communication systems you use:

- *Student mailboxes/teacher mailbox.* You and your students can leave notes for one another about assignments, papers due, and makeup work, for example.

- *Student conference.* You can establish a schedule and meet with individual students privately about their progress. All students meet with you, not just failing students.

- *Progress chart.* Give a subject-related progress chart to each student that visually documents the number of assignments completed, scores, and projects, for example.

- *Warnings.* When students are in danger of failing, give them a "red" note.

- *Compliments.* Provide written or verbal acknowledgment of students' quality work.

- *Checklist.* Place a checklist inside daily or weekly folders so that students can see what has been checked by you and approved for credit.

- *Progress list.* Instruct secondary students to maintain their own grades.

- *Midterm progress reports.* Use these reports to list completed assignments and suggestions for improvement.

- *Student-led parent conference.* Have students attend the parent–teacher conference and share their progress with their parents.

- *Other ideas.*

# Classroom and Behavior Management Issues

What are the three most common classroom misbehaviors in your classroom right now? How are you handling each situation? Categorize the issues. Do they relate to routines, student issues, or lack of planning? How can you minimize these disruptions?

| Misbehavior | How It Is Being Handled | How to Avoid It or Minimize It |
|---|---|---|
| 1. | | |
| 2. | | |
| 3. | | |

November

## Looking at Student Work

What are your expectations for your students? What do you expect your students to know and be able to do? How do these expectations relate to the district standards?

What are you looking for in your assignments?

Bring several samples of *one* student's work to a new-teacher support group meeting. Share these samples with your mentor or other new teachers. Ask them to determine and share the "story" of this student's learning.

| What Does This Work Say about This Student? | What Is the Evidence of That? | What Is the Next Learning Step for This Student? |
| --- | --- | --- |
| | | |

Discuss with your mentor why it is important to use data and evidence to make decisions about students.

# Communicating with Parents

### Progress Reports and Report Cards

Discuss the school and district systems for reporting pupil progress. Are there standard formats that are used? Are progress reports done on a computer? Are report cards done on a computer? Also discuss informal systems teachers may use for sharing progress with parents.

### *Formal Communication*

Review the forms you need to complete to communicate progress to parents. Ask your mentor to share personal tips for completing forms easily. If a narrative is required on a report card, review samples of narratives your mentor has written. Remember to check spelling and grammar in all formal communications. Partner up with another new teacher so you can read each other's comments before you give them to parents.

### *Informal Teacher Communication*

- *Between formal progress reports.*  Sometimes there is a need to contact parents between the formal cycle. Students who were failing may be doing well, and you need to let the parents know that their support made a difference. Parents may want to check in to determine whether their child is doing better, because they may want to know whether they should continue to monitor them at home. Share the formats you have used to communicate progress with other new teachers and your mentor. Do you use a checklist? Ask the parents how they would like you to do it. They may have some new ideas about this.

- *Students who are failing.*  If a student fails a test or a major project, it is usually a good idea to tell the parents. Some teachers send the test home and require a signature so the parents can see what was missed. If a meeting is required, then the parents know exactly what the meeting is about and the student can also be present.

- *The notebook.*  Many teachers use a notebook that goes with the student, from home to school, every day or once a week. This communication from parents to teacher maintains an open line of communication.

*November*

## New-Teacher Needs

What do you need this month?

How can you get support?

List some possible people who can help you.

## ● REFLECTions

**Directions:** Complete as many of the bubble prompts as you like after you have finished the activities in the chapter and before you set goals. Add your own prompts to blank bubbles if the prompts listed do not meet your needs. Compare and share your reflections with your mentor and other new teachers at a scheduled meeting.

Something that is really working is . . .

I continue to be challenged by . . .

I need help . . .

My class is . . .

November

## ● SET GOALS Based on Your Needs for Next Month's Reflection and Discussion

**Directions:**

1. Review the pages in this chapter to determine what you need to revisit next month. Use these pages for possible goal ideas. Revisit any of these topics in your new-teacher support group or with your mentor.

2. Use the following to reflect on your anticipated needs. How can your mentor or other new teachers help you?

---

### Two New-Teacher Needs I Have Right Now!

1. _____

_____

_____

2. _____

_____

_____

### My Mentor Can Assist Me in Meeting These Needs

My mentor can assist me in meeting need 1 by . . . _____

_____

My mentor can assist me in meeting need 2 by . . . _____

_____

### My New-Teacher Support Group Can Assist Me

My support group can assist me in meeting need 1 by . . . _____

_____

My support group can assist me in meeting need 2 by . . . _____

_____

# December

*A good teacher is someone who listens to you as a student and always tries to challenge you.* —Fifth-Grade Student

# Maintaining Balance

## Teaching and Keeping the Students Interested

**New-Teacher Phase:** Can I Do This?

*"I'm having trouble keeping the students on task, and I am losing valuable teaching time."*

## INTASC Principles

Review previous discussions of principles in September through November, and review INTASC Principle 4.

● **Principle 4  Instructional Strategies/Problem Solving**
The teacher understands and uses a variety of instructional strategies to encourage students' development of critical thinking, problem solving, and performance skills.

## Maintaining Balance

### Teaching and Keeping the Students Interested

Students know good teachers. Like the fifth-grade quote on the previous page says, "A good teacher is someone who listens to you as a student and always tries to challenge you." In this high-tech world, it is a challenge to keep students' attention. If you don't know what students are capable of doing, you may give your students work that is too easy and then they get bored. Students want to be challenged and want to succeed. Find ways of implementing a variety of strategies that will forward student learning. Listen to the students to find out what they like to learn and how they learn best. The curriculum can be so overwhelming that you just want to "get it done" and move on, forgetting that students need to be at the center of any curriculum work if you want them to learn.

If you are thinking, "Can I do this?" you need to ask your mentor to help you by allowing you to observe what effective strategies look like in the classroom. Maintaining your balance in December is important. What is your "tipping point" this month? Be aware that this is the time of the year when you will feel stressed out. Expect that and try to focus on things that will support you. Have some fun!

Review the entire chapter to see what you would like to focus on this month. Use all these process pages as a guide to enrich the quality of your monthly mentoring conversations with your mentor or other new teachers.

## ● Journal Entry

**Directions:** Read the cover page and the narrative for this month. How does this month's topic, the quotes, phase, and narrative overview relate to you right now? Are you comfortable with this topic? Do you need some help? How are you feeling right now?

Use your journal to record your thoughts, feelings, and questions in a free-flowing narrative. This page is for your personal reflection; it does not need to be shared as a written document. You are, however, encouraged to share excerpts with other new teachers or with your mentor as needed.

## Reflections:

*Today . . .*

Date _____

## ● PLAN Being Mentored . . . In Action!

### Questions for Participating in a Quality Conversation

Participating in a mentoring conversation requires you to be fully engaged. It requires listening and being open to what your mentor is sharing. This means you need to think about the questions you have and how to ask them. It does not mean you have to copy exactly what your mentor recommends, but it does mean you will reflect on the conversations and think about what makes sense for you.

Other new teachers have had these questions in December. Check the questions that you would like to discuss with your mentor or other new teachers in your school or district.

**New Teachers' Possible Questions:**

_____ What does the district expect of me as a first year teacher?

_____ Can you help me select a variety of strategies that will work for me?

_____ I need help incorporating problem solving into my lessons. What should I do?

_____ Critical thinking is important, but I have to cover so much content. How can I incorporate that skill into my lessons?

_____ What are the successful strategies you have used that encourage students to think?

_____ I am losing track of the other INTASC Principles we covered from September to November. There is so much to know. Can you review them with me?

_____ Other questions I have . . .

## ● Be Prepared

### Your Mentor May Also Ask You Questions!

**Mentor's Possible Questions:**

_____ What is working for you right now in your classroom?

_____ When are your students most interested in learning?

_____ What do you most enjoy about teaching and why do you think that is so?

_____ What can I do to assist you right now that would reduce your anxiety?

## ● Monthly Organizer

### *What I Need to Do Each Month*

**Maintaining Balance:**
**Teaching and Keeping the Students Interested**

*December*

| *Pages in this month's chapter help me to . . .* | | |
|---|---|---|
| **PLAN** | Read the title page quotes and standards | page 113 |
| | Read the narrative page | page 114 |
| | Read "Plan Your Time Wisely" | page 118 |
| | Complete the calendar with meeting dates | page 119 |
| **CONNECT** | Review connections | page 120 |
| | Connect with other new teachers | page 120 |
| **ACT** | Review the list of choices | page 121 |
| | Complete the pages you selected | pages 124–130 |
| **REFLECT** | Complete your journal entry | page 115 |
| | Fill in the bubbles | page 131 |
| **SET GOALS** | What's next for you? | page 132 |

## ● PLAN Your Time Wisely

### *What Is Important to You?*

As a new teacher, you will quickly discover you don't seem to have enough time to do it all! Planning your time wisely is crucial to your success in the classroom. Schedule meetings with your mentor and other new teachers early, and put the dates and times in your planning calendar. Make these meetings a priority each month.

- Meetings with your mentor or colleagues may be held before, during, or after school.

- Schedule personal quiet time for yourself to reflect and write in this guide so you can capture your feelings, ideas, and modifications for teaching each month. You can't remember everything, and writing in this guide will document your practice so you can use this as a guide during your second year of teaching.

- Schedule time to read the pages in this guidebook that relate to you. Skim the entire book so you are familiar with the topics. It is OK to skip around or read all the classroom management pages first! Use the monthly topics as a guide for group discussions with other new or experienced teachers, or with your mentor.

### *Location and Time for Meetings*

Use the key at the bottom of the calendar page to indicate the time of your meeting and place it on the calendar along with the time, length of meeting, and location. Select a private location for meetings with your mentor or colleagues. Make sure you select a place where you will not be interrupted. Meetings may range from five minutes to an hour! What works for you will depend on what you need and what the focus of the meeting is for that day.

What else could you include on your calendar to keep yourself organized?

- Faculty meetings
- Parent conferences
- Professional development workshops

---

*What Do I Need to Be Successful Right Now?*

---

# December Calendar

| MONDAY | TUESDAY | WEDNESDAY | THURSDAY | FRIDAY |
|--------|---------|-----------|----------|--------|
| | | | | |
| | | | | |
| | | | | |
| | | | | |
| | | | | |

December

Key: B = Before school  D = During the day (preparation time or lunchtime)  A = After school

## ● CONNECT with People, Readings, Professional Associations, Resources, and Technology

▶ *What are the resources that exist in your school and community that could assist you in maintaining balance and engaging students?*

**Directions:**

1. Review your journal entry and questions from the PLAN Being Mentored . . . In Action! page for this month.

2. How can you *connect* with people in your school or district, readings, professional associations, resources, or technology to help you? You may complete this page by yourself, with your mentor, or with a group of new teachers.

### CONNECT *with People . . .*

Who in the school building (experienced teachers, other beginning teachers, custodians, secretaries, etc.) may be able to help with December needs?

What agencies in the community relate to the topics *instructional strategies* and *problem solving?*

How can parents be helpful this month?

**Names:**

### CONNECT *with Readings, Professional Associations, and Resources . . .*

What have you read or used that would assist you in using a variety of instructional strategies to develop critical-thinking, problem-solving, and performance skills? You may refer to student teaching courses and readings. Your mentor may have books that relate to this topic.

**Titles:**

### CONNECT *with Technology . . .*

Find websites and links that will provide information about

- Instructional strategies for your grade level
- Problem-solving ideas for teachers
- Critical thinking
- Teaching for understanding
- Making content meaningful at the _____ grade level

**Websites:**

## ● ACTIVITIES: Select Topics for Reflection and Discussion

### *What Should I Be Thinking about in December?*

This list of activities requires you to ACT either by reflecting on a topic or discussing the topic with your mentor, other experienced teachers, or other new teachers. These activities are designed to stimulate your thinking. Write in this book so you will have a documentation of your thoughts and ideas for next year's planning. You do not have to complete all activities.

**December**

### Maintaining Balance:
### Teaching and Keeping the Students Interested

| | **FIRST STEP:** Start the month with a new-teacher support group meeting! | |
|---|---|---|
| **✓** | **Check the ACTivities from the following list that are most meaningful for you to discuss.** | **Page** |
| | ACT 1    Revisiting Behavior Management | 124 |
| | ACT 2    Avoiding Common Problems and Keeping Students Interested | 125 |
| | ACT 3    When Is It Time to Seek Additional Support? | 126 |
| | ACT 4    Problem Solving and Critical Thinking | 127 |
| | ACT 5    Classroom and Behavior Management Issues | 128 |
| | ACT 6    Looking at Student Work | 129 |
| | ACT 7    Communicating with Parents | 130 |

## ● FIRST STEP:  Host a New-Teacher Support Group Meeting

*Have snacks and water or soft drinks available. Hold the meeting in one of your classrooms so you can see teacher ideas in action. Rotate the classroom so you all have a chance to show and tell what you are doing. The host teacher could lead the meeting. Put a colorful sign on your door that says "New-Teacher Meeting. Please do not disturb." You may also want to invite other experienced teachers in the building or district who are also interested in sharing ideas. Set ground rules so everyone has a chance to talk. Use this monthly topic as a guide to keep you focused. Assign a timekeeper and set the next meeting date!*

**First:** Welcome and introduce everyone. Take some time to go around the room and quickly share your name and grade level, and one thing that is going really well!

**Then:** Review your November new-teacher REFLECTions bubbles from this guide. If you haven't completed the bubbles, do it now, then discuss what you wrote and how you can help each other.

**Next:** Review the SET GOALS page that you completed after the November support group meeting. How will you meet these goals?

**Begin:** Discuss one or more topics from the ACTivities pages for this month. Which topic do most of you need to discuss right now?

**Network:** Complete the CONNECTion page together.

**Acknowledge:** Recognize what you have done so far this year and, instead of focusing on what you don't know, acknowledge your successes! Remind the group to complete the REFLECTion and SET GOALS pages on their own. The last day of the month is a good time to reflect.

**Share:** End the session with compliments for each other and at least one practical idea for December. Take time to complete the Notes page and set a date for next month's sharing group.

## Notes

Something I learned in the group today . . .

Something I will use in my classroom from this meeting . . .

Questions I have to . . .

    Ask my mentor . . .

    Ask other new teachers . . .

    Ask administrators . . .

Idea to share at the next meeting . . .

# Revisiting Behavior Management

At this point in the year, you may be having some difficulty. You certainly will be tired, and you might need to review the basics. Take some time to go back to August orientation ideas and ask your mentor how to deal with disruptive behaviors that may be occurring in your classroom.

Take a deep breath and review your discipline and behavior management philosophy. How are you responding to inappropriate behavior and why are you responding that way?

What is your discipline philosophy? How does it compare with the other new teachers'? Describe an incident that has occurred and show how it could be handled two different ways depending on the teacher's philosophy.

Incident: _____

One way to respond:

_____

_____

_____

_____

_____

_____

Another way to respond:

_____

_____

_____

_____

_____

_____

Discuss positive, appropriate ways to deal with recurring misbehavior.

# Avoiding Common Problems and Keeping Students Interested

Review these key areas that could lead to discipline problems.

- *Classroom management.* Have you structured your classroom in an orderly way to avoid potential problems? Traffic flow? Room setup? What could you change to avoid any further issues?

- *Lesson planning.* Have you designed lessons that meet the needs of all students so they don't get frustrated and angry? Are the lessons challenging but doable? Do you have accommodations for grouping that avoid discipline issues? How can you redesign lessons to avoid future discipline problems you are experiencing?

- *Discipline—rules, rewards, and consequences.* Are the rules clearly posted and understood? Do students "own" them or are they imposed on them? Are you consistent when you apply the consequences? Do you treat all students fairly? What do you need to do to be sure your rules, rewards, and consequences are working to avoid problems?

## Keep Track of What Is Working!

It is so easy to stay focused on the one student who is gaining all the attention in your classroom. You certainly want everyone to behave and listen to you. Don't forget, you are doing many things right! List the behaviors you are observing in your classroom that are positive and list why you think they are working. What are you doing to maintain that behavior? Keep it up!

| Classroom Behavior | What You Are Doing | Why Is It Working? |
|---|---|---|
| Class is passing in papers in an orderly way every day with their names on them! | Stopping class three minutes before the bell to allow time to pass in papers. | Consistently ask students to check their names and pass in papers. |
|  |  |  |
|  |  |  |
|  |  |  |

December

## When Is It Time to Seek Additional Support?

Sometimes students need more help than you can provide. It is not your fault when students come to school with issues that are beyond repair in a classroom setting. Some students need medical and psychological help, and you need to know when to get it. As a new teacher, you should consult with your mentor to get the appropriate assistance for the student.

How do you know when you need more help?

- When you have exhausted your possibilities.

- When the student exhibits serious problems beyond the scope of common issues.

- When your mentor has determined the student needs additional help.

- When parents have indicated a need for support.

What should new teachers do?

- Maintain accurate records of all misbehaviors with dates of offenses.

- Write a request for help with your mentor.

How do new teachers know they haven't failed?

- They have tried a number of approaches with the student and documented them.

- Their mentor teacher has advised the student needs additional help.

From Pelletier, Carol Marra. *Strategies For Successful Student Teaching: A Comprehensive Guide*, 2/e. Published by Allyn and Bacon, Boston, MA. Copyright © 2004 by Pearson Education. Reprinted by permission of the publisher.

# Problem Solving and Critical Thinking

Ask your mentor to discuss the strategies he or she has used to enhance students' problem-solving abilities. If you are a secondary teacher, how do these strategies relate to your content? Solving problems engages learners. What problem-solving strategies are you using in your classroom?

Critical thinking allows students to go beyond the basic memorization and to *engage* with the content. Ask your mentor to share her critical thinking strategies with you.

Performance skills are natural ways for students to share what they know and are able to do with what they know. Students enjoy plays, reading poetry, writing original stories, drawing, and dancing. Discuss ways in which these important skills can be integrated into daily lessons and units. List examples here:

Think about and discuss how problem-solving, critical-thinking, and performance skills can reduce behavior problems.

**December**

# Classroom and Behavior Management Issues

## Classroom and School Problems

Discuss recurring problems with your mentor regarding individual students or the whole class. Review the four problem categories listed here and identify the issues. Are these solutions appropriate options? Add your own ideas.

| Problems | What You Need to Do |
|---|---|
| *Chronic work avoidance*<br>Evidenced, for example, by being absent regularly, fooling around in class, not passing in assignments, tardiness. | • Make sure student is capable of work.<br>• Keep accurate records of what is missing.<br>• Talk with mentor teacher.<br>• Let student know how assignments affect grade.<br>• Talk with parents.<br>• Other? |
| *Habitual rule breaking*<br>Evidenced, for example, by calling out in class, not bringing a pencil to class regularly, being talkative, forgetting other materials. | • Use consequences established.<br>• Try behavior modification systems.<br>• Talk with student privately.<br>• Discuss issue with mentor teacher.<br>• Talk with parents.<br>• Other? |
| *Hostile verbal outbursts*<br>Evidenced, for example, by angry and loud yelling, chip-on-the-shoulder attitude, defiance when asked to complete assignments. | • Determine whether the outburst is just momentary.<br>• Don't engage in a power struggle.<br>• Remove the student if anger persists.<br>• Talk with mentor teacher.<br>• Talk with principal.<br>• Talk with guidance counselor.<br>• Talk with parents.<br>• Other? |
| *Fighting, destruction, weapons, alcohol or drug abuse*<br>Evidenced, for example, by hallway pushing, violence with peers, threats, glazed look in class. | • Send a student for help.<br>• Disperse crowds that may gather to watch.<br>• Talk calmly; do not shout or scream.<br>• Report the incident immediately.<br>• Other? |

From Pelletier, Carol Marra. *Strategies For Successful Student Teaching: A Comprehensive Guide*, 2/e. Published by Allyn and Bacon, Boston, MA. Copyright © 2004 by Pearson Education. Reprinted by permission of the publisher.

## Looking at Student Work

### Using Criteria to Assess Performance

Think about and discuss with your mentor or other new teachers the indicators of success for student work. How do you know your students have learned? How do you use data to analyze student work? Designing rubrics and making lists of indicators of success allow you to use concrete evidence to demonstrate progress. What are the district expectations for learning?

Randomly select a sample of student work from a completed set of papers and discuss how it fits into one of the following categories:

| Below Standard | Meets the Standard | Above Standard |
|---|---|---|
| What indicates that it is below standard? Be specific in your discussion. | What evidence shows this work meets the standard? Check the indicators. | What makes you say it is above the standard? Be specific. |

Now look at the whole set of completed papers from the whole class. Sort the papers into these categories.

| Below Standard | Meets the Standard | Above Standard |
|---|---|---|
| How many papers here? _____  <br><br> % of class _____ | How many papers here?_____  <br><br> % of class _____ | How many papers here?_____  <br><br> % of class _____ |

Why is this an important activity? What did you learn from doing this?

*December*

# Communicating with Parents

## Complimentary Phone Calls and Positive Notes

One sure way to keep students interested in school is to compliment them for what they are doing right! Parents and students love to hear good news. Because the school day is so hectic and the needs of failing students have to be a priority for a new teacher, there often is not time to compliment the students who are doing well. Discuss the ways you can systematically let students and parents know they are progressing. Two ideas here will get your discussion started.

### *Complimentary Phone Calls*

The idea is that every student in the class will get a compliment for something in December. You can think of this as a holiday gift to the student and the parents. Make a few phone calls each night and leave a message on the voicemail/answering machine or speak personally to the parents. More than one compliment call can be made in a night. No one gets two calls until everyone in the class is called once. The sample message script is as follows:

> This is an official *complimentary phone call* from Mr. Correiro, Susan's teacher at Sunnyside School. I am calling to compliment your daughter for her outstanding work in class this week. She worked with other students who needed help, she answered questions in class, and she did very well on her project. Please let Susan know that she received this compliment. Have a great day.

You should not get into long conversations with parents at this time. This is not a conference; it is a compliment for something very specific. This call is *brief* so that this activity can fit into your busy day.

### *Positive Notes*

This compliment could be given electronically as an email or ecard or you could send a *compliment postcard*. The key is to be specific about what is being complimented so the student is clear about what positive behavior or academic performance is. The goal for you is to identify good behavior and reward it by telling the parents.

Again, the goal is to compliment every student in the class in December. Some will be more challenging than others, but every student is doing something right. The next morning in class after their first compliment calls, you will notice students' responses.

From Pelletier, Carol M. *Mentoring In Action: A Month-by-Month Curriculum For Mentors And Their New Teachers*, 1/e. Published by Allyn and Bacon, Boston, MA. Copyright © 2006 by Pearson Education. Reprinted by permission of the publisher.

## ● REFLECTions

**Directions:** Complete as many of the bubble prompts as you like after you have finished the activities in the chapter and before you set goals. Add your own prompts to blank bubbles if the prompts listed do not meet your needs. Compare and share your reflections with your mentor and other new teachers at a scheduled meeting.

I am frustrated by . . .

I need to . . .

I really love . . .

The best way to describe this year so far is . . .

December

## ● SET GOALS Based on Your Needs for Next Month's Reflection and Discussion

**Directions:**

1. Review the pages in this chapter to determine what you need to revisit next month. Use these pages for possible goal ideas. Revisit any of these topics in your new-teacher support group or with your mentor.

2. Use the following to reflect on your anticipated needs. How can your mentor or other new teachers help you?

| Two New-Teacher Needs I Have Right Now! |
|---|
| 1. _____<br><br>_____<br><br>_____<br><br>2. _____<br><br>_____<br><br>_____ |

| My Mentor Can Assist Me in Meeting These Needs |
|---|
| My mentor can assist me in meeting need 1 by . . . _____<br><br>_____<br><br>My mentor can assist me in meeting need 2 by . . . _____<br><br>_____ |

| My New-Teacher Support Group Can Assist Me |
|---|
| My support group can assist me in meeting need 1 by . . . _____<br><br>_____<br><br>My support group can assist me in meeting need 2 by . . . _____<br><br>_____ |

# January

*I think patience makes a good teacher.* —Second-Grade Student

# Beginning a
# New Calendar Year
## Looking Back
## and Moving Forward

### New-Teacher Phase: Refreshed and Ready

*"I want to start the year over again
because I know so much more now."*

---

## INTASC Principles

Review INTASC Principle 9 with your mentor.

● **Principle 9  Professional Growth/Reflection**
The teacher is a reflective practitioner who continually evaluates the effects
of his or her choices and actions on others (students, parents, and other
professionals in the learning community) and who actively seeks out
opportunities to grow professionally.

# Beginning a New Calendar Year
## Looking Back and Moving Forward

Patience does make a good teacher, just like the second-grade student says in the quote on the previous page. Be patient with yourself. You can't learn everything in one year. If your mentor makes it look easy, don't compare yourself. You are growing and developing with each new experience and interaction with your students. Sometimes you are moving so quickly you don't even see what you are learning.

The beginning of a new year is a perfect opportunity to look back to what you did in August and to look ahead to what you plan for June. Ask your mentor to be the guide you need to see the light at the end of the year. Read your REFLECTion pages and review your notes in this book. Congratulate yourself!

Are you refreshed and ready to begin or are you looking cautiously at the rest of the year? Use this month to get grounded in what you are doing well and continue to reflect. Do some New Year's goal setting. New Year's resolutions are fun to make and easy to break. Design doable, measurable goals with your mentor and other new teachers.

A professional portfolio may be required in your district or state. If it is, these pages (beginning this month from January to June) will keep you and the other new teachers on track for completing it. Use all these process pages as a guide to enrich the quality of your monthly mentoring conversations and your own personal reflection.

## ● Journal Entry

**Directions:** Read the cover page and the narrative for this month. How does this month's topic, the quotes, phase, and narrative overview relate to you right now? Are you comfortable with this topic? Do you need some help? How are you feeling right now?

Use your journal to record your thoughts, feelings, and questions in a free-flowing narrative. This page is for your personal reflection; it does not need to be shared as a written document. You are, however, encouraged to share excerpts with other new teachers or with your mentor as needed.

### Reflections:

*Today . . .*

January

Date _____

## ● PLAN Being Mentored . . . In Action!

### Questions for Participating in a Quality Conversation

Participating in a mentoring conversation requires you to be fully engaged. It requires listening and being open to what your mentor is sharing. This means you need to think about the questions you have and how to ask them. It does not mean you have to copy exactly what your mentor recommends, but it does mean you will reflect on the conversations and think about what makes sense for you.

Other new teachers have had these questions in January. Check the questions that you would like to discuss with your mentor or other new teachers in your school or district.

### New Teachers' Possible Questions:

_____ I would like to share ideas and learn from others. How do I connect with other new teachers?

_____ What opportunities are available in the district, through the teachers' union or from local professional development providers?

_____ In your professional opinion, what should I focus on to improve my practice for the rest of the year?

_____ Is there a way I could easily connect with the parents and the community that would assist me in my teaching?

_____ Do you have any suggestions for assisting me in reflecting more systematically so I don't lose my good ideas?

_____ Other questions I have . . .

## ● Be Prepared

### Your Mentor May Also Ask You Questions!

### Mentor's Possible Questions:

_____ Do you keep a journal? Why or why not? How do you reflect on your practice?

_____ Are you a member of a professional organization?

_____ What changes have you already made in what you are doing and why?

_____ What can I do to assist you right now that would reduce your anxiety?

## ● Monthly Organizer

### *What I Need to Do Each Month*

**Beginning a New Calendar Year:**
**Looking Back and Moving Forward**

**January**

## ● PLAN Your Time Wisely

### What Is Important to You?

As a new teacher, you will quickly discover you don't seem to have enough time to do it all! Planning your time wisely is crucial to your success in the classroom. Schedule meetings with your mentor and other new teachers early, and put the dates and times in your planning calendar. Make these meetings a priority each month.

- Meetings with your mentor or colleagues may be held before, during, or after school.

- Schedule personal quiet time for yourself to reflect and write in this guide so you can capture your feelings, ideas, and modifications for teaching each month. You can't remember everything, and writing in this guide will document your practice so you can use this as a guide during your second year of teaching.

- Schedule time to read the pages in this guidebook that relate to you. Skim the entire book so you are familiar with the topics. It is OK to skip around or read all the classroom management pages first! Use the monthly topics as a guide for group discussions with other new or experienced teachers, or with your mentor.

### Location and Time for Meetings

Use the key at the bottom of the calendar page to indicate the time of your meeting and place it on the calendar along with the time, length of meeting, and location. Select a private location for meetings with your mentor or colleagues. Make sure you select a place where you will not be interrupted. Meetings may range from five minutes to an hour! What works for you will depend on what you need and what the focus of the meeting is for that day.

What else could you include on your calendar to keep yourself organized?

- Faculty meetings
- Parent conferences
- Professional development workshops

***What Do I Need to Be Successful Right Now?***

# January Calendar

| MONDAY | TUESDAY | WEDNESDAY | THURSDAY | FRIDAY |
|---|---|---|---|---|
| | | | | |
| | | | | |
| | | | | |
| | | | | |
| | | | | |

January

Key: B = Before school   D = During the day (preparation time or lunchtime)   A = After school

## ● CONNECT with People, Readings, Professional Associations, Resources, and Technology

> ▶ *What are the resources that exist in your school and community that could assist you in looking back and moving forward?*

**Directions:**

1. Review your journal entry and questions from the PLAN Being Mentored . . . In Action! page for this month.

2. How can you *connect* with people in your school or district, readings, professional associations, resources, or technology to help you? You may complete this page by yourself, with your mentor, or with a group of new teachers.

### CONNECT *with People . . .*

Who in the school building (experienced teachers, other beginning teachers, custodians, secretaries, etc.) may be able to help with January needs?

Who in the professional community or district inspires professional growth and reflection?

How could parents be helpful in reflecting on the past few months and looking forward?

**Names:**

### CONNECT *with Readings, Professional Associations, and Resources . . .*

What have you read or used that could assist in reflection and goal setting for the new calendar year? You may refer to student teaching courses and readings. Your mentor may have books that relate to this topic.

**Titles:**

### CONNECT *with Technology . . .*

Find websites and links that will provide information about

- Teacher reflection
- Goal setting for the second half of the year
- Reflective practice
- Writing about practice
- Professional development

**Websites:**

## ● ACTIVITIES: Select Topics for Reflection and Discussion

### *What Should I Be Thinking about in January?*

This list of activities requires you to ACT either by reflecting on a topic or discussing the topic with your mentor, other experienced teachers, or other new teachers. These activities are designed to stimulate your thinking. You do not have to complete all of them! Write in this book so you will have documentation of your thoughts and ideas for next year's planning.

### Beginning a New Calendar Year: Looking Back and Moving Forward

| | **FIRST STEP:** Start the month with a new-teacher support group meeting! | |
|---|---|---|
| **✓** | **Check the ACTivities from the following list that are most meaningful for you to discuss.** | **Page** |
| | ACT 1    Looking Back | 144 |
| | ACT 2    Moving Forward | 145 |
| | ACT 3    What Do I Believe? | 146 |
| | ACT 4    Constructing a Sociogram | 147 |
| | ACT 5    Social Activities and a Sense of Humor! | 148 |
| | ACT 6    Classroom and Behavior Management Issues | 149 |
| | ACT 7    Looking at Student Work | 150 |
| | ACT 8    Communicating with Parents | 151 |
| | ACT 9    Preparing a Professional Portfolio | 152 |

January

## ● FIRST STEP:  Host a New-Teacher Support Group Meeting

*Have snacks and water or soft drinks available. Hold the meeting in one of your classrooms so you can see teacher ideas in action. Rotate the classroom so you all have a chance to show and tell what you are doing. The host teacher could lead the meeting. Put a colorful sign on your door that says "New-Teacher Meeting. Please do not disturb." You may also want to invite other experienced teachers in the building or district who are also interested in sharing ideas. Set ground rules so everyone has a chance to talk. Use this monthly topic as a guide to keep you focused. Assign a timekeeper and set the next meeting date!*

**First:**  Welcome and introduce everyone. Take some time to go around the room and quickly share your name and grade level, and one thing that is going really well!

**Then:**  Review your December new-teacher REFLECTion bubbles from this guide. If you haven't completed the bubbles, do it now, then discuss what you wrote and how you can help each other.

**Next:**  Review the SET GOALS page that you completed after the December support group meeting. How will you meet these goals?

**Begin:**  Discuss one or more topics from the ACTivities pages for this month. Which topic do most of you need to discuss right now?

**Network:**  Complete the CONNECTion page together.

**Acknowledge:**  Recognize what you have done so far this year and, instead of focusing on what you don't know, acknowledge your successes! Remind the group to complete the REFLECTion and SET GOALS pages on their own. The last day of the month is a good time to reflect.

**Share:**  End the session with compliments for each other and at least one practical idea for January. Take time to complete the Notes page and set a date for next month's sharing group.

## *Notes*

Something I learned in the group today . . .

Something I will use in my classroom from this meeting . . .

Questions I have to . . .

  Ask my mentor . . .

  Ask other new teachers . . .

  Ask administrators . . .

Idea to share at the next meeting . . .

## Looking Back

Reflect on your successes and challenges. What was most difficult for you? What gave you the most joy so far this year? Use these two writing prompts to move you forward. Place your letters in this book for review at the end of the year. Be sure to date them.

**Directions:** Write a letter to yourself that highlights areas of growth, new insights about teaching and learning, and successes. Also include one challenge you are facing that you would like to discuss with your mentor. Lastly, note what you would like to be acknowledged for so far this year. Share your letter with your mentor and other new teachers. Celebrate your growth and set goals for the rest of the year.

List what you will include in your letter here:

**Directions:** Write a journal entry from the perspective of the most difficult student in the classroom. Imagine an assignment has been given to the class that all the students write about their own lives, school, how they are doing right now, and something that is going on.

List what you will include in your letter here:

This is a very powerful process and is especially enlightening when shared with other new teachers. Ask your mentor to assist you in discovering the issues about this student so that the behavior may be seen differently.

# Moving Forward

Share the successes you wrote about in your letter with your mentor and other new teachers. Don't take your struggles personally and don't worry if you haven't handled every student perfectly. Work with your mentor to dissect the problems you have and make them more manageable and measurable. All problems cannot be solved. There are some things teachers cannot change about students' lives. Let go of the first half of the year and begin again. What is your New Year's resolution?

### What Are You Worried About? Problems to Possibilities

Try this process in your new-teacher support group or with your mentor:

1. Write your most challenging problems or worries on a *blue* sticky note (symbolizes what makes the new teacher "blue"). Work together to classify the problem in a category (such as student misbehavior, managing paper, organizing the room, parent issue) and write that on the top of the blue sticky note. Share the problems with each other. Adapt categories as needed to make common categories understood by all new teachers. Complete as many "worries" as you want. Mentors also have worries and may participate!

2. Place the problems on the Worry Wall at the front of the room in categories as defined by the classification at the top of the sticky note.

3. Everyone should then walk up to the wall and read all the problems and think about the possible solutions to them. Using *yellow* sticky notes, place possible solutions to these problems. Provide multiple solutions to as many problems as you want.

4. The teachers who originally placed the problems on the wall should now go back and pick them up along with the solutions attached to them. Talk in pairs about what possibilities were generated and how they can be implemented.

*January*

## What Do I Believe?

At this time of year, it is important for you to revisit the philosophy statements you may have written in college. What do you believe about teaching and learning? Has it changed? Why or why not? Do this process alone, with your mentor, or with your new-teacher support group.

**Directions:**  Complete the following questions. First list three words that describe you as a teacher:

1. _____

2. _____

3. _____

Then, list three words your students would use to describe you as a teacher:

1. _____

2. _____

3. _____

How do these compare? Why are they alike or different? Share.

Now think about your beliefs about teaching and learning. Complete the following prompts twice:

I believe . . .

I also believe . . .

Last, list *one* way you are demonstrating what you believe in the classroom. What are you *doing* that shows what you believe or who you are (as described in your descriptive words)? Set goals that relate to your beliefs:

## Constructing a Sociogram

Construct a sociogram to gather information about what the students believe for-wards their learning. Draw the relationships on a piece of paper after you collect the data so you can see who the stars and isolates are in the classroom.

**Directions:**

1. Ask students in the classroom to list three students, by first, second, and third choice, with whom they would prefer to work in the classroom. (Make a distinction between work partners and social partners outside of school.) Tell them it is for possible future group projects and that you may use it to try and create teams with at least one person they prefer to work with.

2. Have the students write why they selected each student. This will give you some insight, and themes may repeat themselves.

3. Collect the data and make a grid with students' names across the top and down the left side. Graph paper works well. Place a 1, 2, or 3 under the student's name as indicated to show choices.

| Sample Sociogram | | | | |
|---|---|---|---|---|
|  | *Kas* | *Carlos* | *Germaine* | *Olga* |
| Kas | — | 1 | 3 | 2 |
| Carlos | 3 | — | 1 | 2 |
| Germaine | 3 | 2 | — | 1 |
| Olga | 3 | 2 | 1 | — |

4. Tally choices to indicate most preferred working partners (commonly called *stars*) and least selected working partners (referred to as *isolates*).

January

# Social Activities and a Sense of Humor!

Most of your meetings so far this year are probably spent trying to resolve issues, share challenges, and discuss problems. Even though there is a place for acknowledgment, it often gets buried by pressing emotional worries you bring to the table. Make this activity just about *fun*. What might you enjoy doing socially? Do you want to have a school social? A reception? A party? A movie night? What would be good for you and other new teachers right now? Ask your mentor to assist you in finding space, resources, and the time to do this. You do need to connect with other new teachers and find some time to laugh about what is happening in your classrooms. Perhaps you will want to schedule something similar every month. Take time! Make time! Here are some ideas to consider.

### New-Teacher Appreciation Day (or Night or Saturday)

Organize a social event for the new teachers in the district. Perhaps go to a play together, or a show, or just out to dinner. Maybe the school could even pay! This should be social, fun, and welcoming.

### Social Life Survival Directory

Find out where to go for great meals or social interaction. You have been so busy teaching, you probably have not done many fun things, and many of you might now be complaining that you have "no social life." Ask your mentors to create a *Social Survival Directory* for you!

### Sense of Humor Booklet

Share any funny stories that have happened in your classrooms. Create a list of humorous situations you have encountered and share them! Laugh!

Remember that talking about students, their parents, or any other school issue is not appropriate at any event. Everyone has had an experience where you have heard gossip and inappropriate information being transferred about students. Professionalism and confidentiality must be a priority for you as a new teacher. Have fun, but not at others' expense.

# Classroom and Behavior Management Issues

### Typical Situations for Teachers: What Would You Do If . . .

Use the cases on this page to brainstorm possible solutions with your mentor. Make the case fit the grade level you are working with. Expand the details to illustrate what the student would do at that grade level. For example, a sleeping student in case 6 may be handled very differently in an early childhood classroom as opposed to a high school English class. List three possible solutions for each case and try them in your own classes. Discuss what happens at your next meeting.

- *Case 1: The class clown.*  The class clown comes in late and tells jokes every day during class. Everyone loves her and laughs so hard, it is difficult to get their attention. Valuable class time is being wasted.

- *Case 2: The bully.*  This girl hits at least one person a day. She walks by people and punches their arm or she trips anyone who walks by her desk. She is the terror of the playground.

- *Case 3: The lie.*  A very likable student who always completed his homework lied and said he handed it in. You discover he did not do it at all and just called out *yes* when you asked students during roll call.

- *Case 4: A destructive student.*  A very quiet student exhibits aggressive behavior by quietly breaking pencils in her desk while the teacher is giving directions.

- *Case 5: Shouting out.*  This student is so excited and wants to participate in class discussions. She always shouts out the answers when you ask the class general questions. No one else has a chance to talk.

- *Case 6: The sleeper.*  This student slumps over his desk in the back of the room. He is not disturbing anyone, but he is not learning the material either. He is in danger of failing the class.

- *Case 7: The cheater.*  This student was caught cheating on a test. The answers were clearly written on her hand, and she was copying them on to her paper. She had cheated before and said she would not do it again.

- *Case 8: A fist fight.*  Two students hit each other about a personal issue in the hallway outside the teacher's door.

January

# Looking at Student Work

### Identify Patterns

Bring a whole set of completed papers to a meeting or review them by yourself. Sort the papers into the categories presented here or into the categories in the rubric you are using.

| Below Standard | Meets the Standard | Above Standard |
|---|---|---|
| How many papers here?<br><br>% of class _____ | How many papers here?<br><br>% of class _____ | How many papers here?<br><br>% of class _____ |

1. Look at all the papers in the Below Standard category or the lowest category in your rubric. What is the pattern? Are the students making similar mistakes? What could you do to move these students to the Meets the Standard category?

2. Look at all the papers in the Meets the Standard category. What is the pattern? Are the students making similar mistakes? What could you do to move these students to Above Standard?

# Communicating with Parents

### Parent Meetings to Set Goals for the New Year

You will feel a bit more revitalized after a break from school and you will have the energy to set new goals for communicating with parents. Set up meetings with the parents of students you are finding particularly challenging.

### *Sample Meeting Agenda*

1. Opening the meeting
   - I am so glad you could join me today to discuss John's progress.
   - The purpose of this meeting is . . .
   - Can you tell me some things that are going on right now . . .
   - You know your child better than I do; can you give me some insights so I can help him be successful in school?

2. Sharing the positive
   - This is what I see going well for John right now . . .
   - This sample of work shows he can . . .
   - I also know that John is very good at . . .

3. Standards and curriculum goals
   - These are the learning goals for ___ grade this year.
   - Let's look at the areas where John needs assistance . . .
   - By the end of the year John needs to meet ____ standards
   - My concerns for John are . . .

4. Working together to set goals
   - How can we assist John together?
   - One thing you could do at home is . . .
   - When should we meet again to check on John's progress?

*January*

## Preparing a Professional Portfolio

Some districts require new teachers to prepare a portfolio as part of their induction responsibilities for the state requirements for certification. If you do not have to do this as part of the licensing requirement, you may still want to collect a variety of materials you can use to document your year in the classroom. Portfolios are very useful visual displays of actual work and are a demonstration of competency and professional growth. Use the following list as a guide. There is no need to organize these items yet. Every month hereafter there will be a Preparing a Professional Portfolio activity in this book to move you along in the process.

### Inventory of Possible Artifacts for Portfolio

\_\_\_\_ Diagram of classroom (i.e., floor plan, photos, or both)

\_\_\_\_ Lesson plans

\_\_\_\_ Unit plans interrelating subject areas, including the arts, thematic, and others

\_\_\_\_ Cooperative learning techniques

\_\_\_\_ Classroom management and discipline strategies

\_\_\_\_ Samples of student work: each subject area, advanced work, work adapted for diverse needs, homework, tests, artwork, performance assessment

\_\_\_\_ Audiotapes of students in groups; you introducing a lesson

\_\_\_\_ Videotapes (permission required) of students during a lesson, documentary of classroom

\_\_\_\_ Materials from pre-practicum that may be highlighted

\_\_\_\_ Materials from methods course

\_\_\_\_ Photographs of classroom, bulletin boards, group lessons (permission required from students)

\_\_\_\_ Documentation of any honors or awards

\_\_\_\_ Appreciation letters, notes from parents, notes from students

\_\_\_\_ Evaluations from others, mentor teacher recommendation, supervisor evaluation

\_\_\_\_ Professional profile (third-person biographical page) to go with resumé

\_\_\_\_ Books and articles read with how they helped you to be a better teacher

\_\_\_\_ Inspirational writings, poems, or artwork that might serve as titles for pages or cover

\_\_\_\_ Other?

## ● REFLECTions

**Directions:** Reread all the REFLECTions you completed from August through December. Then complete all the bubble prompts here. Share your responses with your mentor and other new teachers at your next scheduled meeting. Combine the responses from all the new teachers and share them anonymously with the mentor coordinator so your voices will be heard.

What I like about the mentor program is . . .

My mentor has helped me . . .

One thing that would make a difference for the rest of the year is . . .

I am really pleased with . . .

I wish the district could . . .

I wish my mentor could . . .

January

## ● SET GOALS Based on Your Needs for Next Month's Reflection and Discussion

**Directions:**

1. Review the pages in this chapter to determine what you need to revisit next month. Use these pages for possible goal ideas. Revisit any of these topics in your new-teacher support group or with your mentor.

2. Use the following to reflect on your anticipated needs. How can your mentor or other new teachers help you?

| Two New-Teacher Needs I Have Right Now! |
|---|
| 1. _____ <br> _____ <br> _____ <br> 2. _____ <br> _____ <br> _____ |
| **My Mentor Can Assist Me in Meeting These Needs** |
| My mentor can assist me in meeting need 1 by . . . _____ <br> _____ <br><br> My mentor can assist me in meeting need 2 by . . . _____ <br> _____ |
| **My New-Teacher Support Group Can Assist Me** |
| My support group can assist me in meeting need 1 by . . . _____ <br> _____ <br><br> My support group can assist me in meeting need 2 by . . . _____ <br> _____ |

*What I think makes a good teacher is that they can teach all kinds of things your parents don't know.* —Sixth-Grade Student

# Engaging Students in the Curriculum

## Focus on Content through Active Inquiry

**New-Teacher Phase:** Staying Focused

*"There is so much to teach before the end of the school year. How will I do it all?"*

## INTASC Principles

Review INTASC Principle 6 with your mentor.

- **Principle 6  Communication/Knowledge**
  The teacher uses knowledge of effective verbal, nonverbal, and media communication techniques to foster active inquiry, collaboration, and supportive interaction in the classroom.

# Engaging Students in the Curriculum
## Focus on Content through Active Inquiry

There is so much to do at this time of year that you might just get very scattered and not know what to do first. Break the curriculum down into bite-size pieces so you can understand what the next steps could be and how you should implement them. The curriculum usually is the most challenging part of the first year because you are teaching it for the first time.

This month highlights the continued use of varied teaching strategies as well as the opportunity to give students choices in the classroom. When a teacher can give options to students about what they can do for homework, for example, the students have to engage in the conversation and commit to something. It is more likely they will actually do their homework if they selected it! Ultimately, it may not matter which homework assignment is completed or how the content is learned.

Communication/Knowledge INTASC Principle 6 will help to focus the discussion on the ways in which you use effective verbal, nonverbal, and media communication techniques to foster active inquiry in your classroom. Ask your mentor to share these valuable strategies with you. What are you doing to engage students in your classroom?

## ● Journal Entry

**Directions:** Read the cover page and the narrative for this month. How does this month's topic, the quotes, phase, and narrative overview relate to you right now? Are you comfortable with this topic? Do you need some help? How are you feeling right now?

Use your journal to record your thoughts, feelings, and questions in a free-flowing narrative. This page is for your personal reflection; it does not need to be shared as a written document. You are, however, encouraged to share excerpts with other new teachers or with your mentor as needed.

---

### Reflections:

*Today . . .*

Date _____

February

## PLAN Being Mentored . . . In Action!
### *Questions for Participating in a Quality Conversation*

Participating in a mentoring conversation requires you to be fully engaged. It requires listening and being open to what your mentor is sharing. This means you need to think about the questions you have and how to ask them. It does not mean you have to copy exactly what your mentor recommends, but it does mean you will reflect on the conversations and think about what makes sense for you.

Other new teachers have had these questions in February. Check the questions that you would like to discuss with your mentor or other new teachers in your school or district.

### New Teachers' Possible Questions:

_____ How do I get the students to support each other and work together?

_____ Are there easy ways to integrate media and audiovisual aids into my lessons?

_____ I want to foster active inquiry in my lessons, but it just gets too complicated. Can you suggest some teachers I could observe who use this technique to engage their students?

_____ I feel like I am talking too much. What are some nonverbal ways I could communicate with my students that will create a supportive environment for learning?

_____ Other questions I have . . .

## Be Prepared
### *Your Mentor May Also Ask You Questions!*

### Mentor's Possible Questions:

_____ What are your goals for creating a collaborative learning environment?

_____ How do you communicate these goals to your students?

_____ What would you do if you could do anything in your classroom right now?

_____ What can I do to assist you right now that would reduce your anxiety?

## ● Monthly Organizer

*What I Need to Do Each Month*

**Engaging Students in the Curriculum:**
**Focus on Content through Active Inquiry**

<table>
<tr><td colspan="3">Pages in this month's chapter help me to . . .</td></tr>
<tr><td rowspan="4">PLAN</td><td>Read the title page quotes and standards</td><td>page 155</td></tr>
<tr><td>Read the narrative page</td><td>page 156</td></tr>
<tr><td>Read "Plan Your Time Wisely"</td><td>page 160</td></tr>
<tr><td>Complete the calendar with meeting dates</td><td>page 161</td></tr>
<tr><td rowspan="2">CONNECT</td><td>Review connections</td><td>page 162</td></tr>
<tr><td>Connect with other new teachers</td><td>page 162</td></tr>
<tr><td rowspan="2">ACT</td><td>Review the list of choices</td><td>page 163</td></tr>
<tr><td>Complete the pages you selected</td><td>pages 166–174</td></tr>
<tr><td rowspan="2">REFLECT</td><td>Complete your journal entry</td><td>page 157</td></tr>
<tr><td>Fill in the bubbles</td><td>page 175</td></tr>
<tr><td>SET GOALS</td><td>What's next for you?</td><td>page 176</td></tr>
</table>

February

## ● PLAN Your Time Wisely

### *What Is Important to You?*

As a new teacher, you will quickly discover you don't seem to have enough time to do it all! Planning your time wisely is crucial to your success in the classroom. Schedule meetings with your mentor and other new teachers early, and put the dates and times in your planning calendar. Make these meetings a priority each month.

- Meetings with your mentor or colleagues may be held before, during, or after school.

- Schedule personal quiet time for yourself to reflect and write in this guide so you can capture your feelings, ideas, and modifications for teaching each month. You can't remember everything, and writing in this guide will document your practice so you can use this as a guide during your second year of teaching.

- Schedule time to read the pages in this guidebook that relate to you. Skim the entire book so you are familiar with the topics. It is OK to skip around or read all the classroom management pages first! Use the monthly topics as a guide for group discussions with other new or experienced teachers, or with your mentor.

### *Location and Time for Meetings*

Use the key at the bottom of the calendar page to indicate the time of your meeting and place it on the calendar along with the time, length of meeting, and location. Select a private location for meetings with your mentor or colleagues. Make sure you select a place where you will not be interrupted. Meetings may range from five minutes to an hour! What works for you will depend on what you need and what the focus of the meeting is for that day.

What else could you include on your calendar to keep yourself organized?

- Faculty meetings
- Parent conferences
- Professional development workshops

---

### *What Do I Need to Be Successful Right Now?*

---

# February Calendar

| MONDAY | TUESDAY | WEDNESDAY | THURSDAY | FRIDAY |
|---|---|---|---|---|
| | | | | |
| | | | | |
| | | | | |
| | | | | |
| | | | | |

Key: B = Before school   D = During the day (preparation time or lunchtime)   A = After school

February

## ● CONNECT with People, Readings, Professional Associations, Resources, and Technology

▶ *What are the resources that exist in your school and community that could assist you in engaging students with the curriculum?*

**Directions:**

1. Review your journal entry and questions from the *PLAN Being Mentored . . . In Action!* page for this month.

2. How can you *connect* with people in your school or district, readings, professional associations, resources, or technology to help you? You may complete this page by yourself, with your mentor, or with a group of new teachers.

### CONNECT *with People . . .*

Who in the school building (experienced teachers, other beginning teachers, custodians, secretaries, etc.) may be able to help with February needs?

Who in the professional community could assist with ideas for communication techniques?

How can parents be used as resources for communication and media techniques?

**Names:**

### CONNECT *with Readings, Professional Associations, and Resources . . .*

What have you read or used that would assist increasing your knowledge of verbal, nonverbal, and media communication techniques to foster active inquiry, collaboration, and supportive interaction in the classroom? You may refer to student teaching courses and readings. Your mentor may have books that relate to this topic.

**Titles:**

### CONNECT *with Technology . . .*

Find websites and links that will provide information about

- Collaboration in the classroom
- Inquiry as a technique for active learning
- The use of media in the classroom

**Websites:**

## ● ACTIVITIES: Select Topics for Reflection and Discussion

### *What Should I Be Thinking about in February?*

This list of activities requires you to ACT by either reflecting on a topic or discussing the topic with your mentor, other experienced teachers, or other new teachers. These activities are designed to stimulate your thinking. You do not have to complete all of them! Write in this book so you will have documentation of your thoughts and ideas for next year's planning.

## Engaging Students in the Curriculum:
## Focus on Content through Active Inquiry

| FIRST STEP: Start the month with a new-teacher support group meeting! | | | |
|---|---|---|---|
| ✓ | Check the ACTivities from the following list that are most meaningful for you to discuss. | | Page |
| | ACT 1 | Using Varied Teaching Strategies | 166 |
| | ACT 2 | Giving Students Choices to Enhance Learning | 167 |
| | ACT 3 | Homework and Opportunities for Enrichment | 168 |
| | ACT 4 | How Much Time? | 169 |
| | ACT 5 | Classroom and Behavior Management Issues | 170 |
| | ACT 6 | Looking at Student Work | 171 |
| | ACT 7 | Communicating with Parents | 172 |
| | ACT 8 | Observing Yourself through Active Listening | 173 |
| | ACT 9 | Preparing a Professional Portfolio | 174 |

**February**

## ● FIRST STEP:  Host a New-Teacher Support Group Meeting

*Have snacks and water or soft drinks available. Hold the meeting in one of your classrooms so you can see teacher ideas in action. Rotate the classroom so you all have a chance to show and tell what you are doing. The host teacher could lead the meeting. Put a colorful sign on your door that says "New-Teacher Meeting. Please do not disturb." You may also want to invite other experienced teachers in the building or district who are also interested in sharing ideas. Set ground rules so everyone has a chance to talk. Use this monthly topic as a guide to keep you focused. Assign a timekeeper and set the next meeting date!*

**First:**   Welcome and introduce everyone. Take some time to go around the room and quickly share your name and grade level and one thing that is going really well!

**Then:**   Review your January new-teacher REFLECTion bubbles from this guide. If you haven't completed the bubbles, do it now, then discuss what you wrote and how you can help each other.

**Next:**   Review the SET GOALS page that you completed after the January support group meeting. How will you meet these goals?

**Begin:**   Discuss one or more topics from the ACTivities pages for this month. Which topic do most of you need to discuss right now?

**Network:**   Complete the CONNECTion page together.

**Acknowledge:**   Recognize what you have done so far this year and, instead of focusing on what you don't know, acknowledge your successes! Remind the group to complete the REFLECTion and SET GOALS pages on their own. The last day of the month is a good time to reflect.

**Share:**   End the session with compliments for each other and at least one practical idea for February. Take time to complete the Notes page and set a date for next month's sharing group.

## *Notes*

Something I learned in the group today . . .

Something I will use in my classroom from this meeting . . .

Questions I have to . . .

   Ask my mentor . . .

   Ask other new teachers . . .

   Ask administrators . . .

Idea to share at the next meeting . . .

February

# Using Varied Teaching Strategies

Think about the ways you are delivering information to students in your classroom. Are you using the strategies on this page? How can you integrate them if you are not using them?

- *Use both auditory and visual directions.* Students in the classroom may be auditory or visual learners. Giving directions in both written and oral forms will include these varied learners. Also, be aware of giving multiple directions, especially orally, that students of varied levels may not be able to retain. Write directions on the board or overhead projector and leave them up throughout an activity so they can be referred to at any time.

- *Demonstrate concepts by using visual examples.* After directions are given and you feel students understand, give specific examples to show concretely what is expected. This does not mean students are supposed to copy the example. This is to provide a visual prop that is used by the teacher to demonstrate what is expected.

- *Allow for choice when appropriate.* If possible, provide several activities that meet the same objective and allow students to choose the one with which they feel most comfortable. For example, if the goal is to solve a word problem in math, choices for solving could include paper and pencil, manipulatives, working alone, or working with a partner. The point is that you want the students to use their best learning style to solve the problem.

- *Plan for varied paces.* Students think and work at different speeds. The faster thinkers are not necessarily the most accurate or the most creative problem solvers. Don't be trapped by rewarding only the quickest students, because you may be missing some outstanding problem solving. Sometimes it is appropriate to leave a task incomplete. Doing a portion of some math problems can show you whether the students understand the concept.

- *Assist students who need support.* Some students will need additional support during a lesson because they do not understand the directions or are unable to complete the task. You may not have time to walk around the room and meet with these students individually. One strategy is to let them work with a partner who is able to explain more clearly what is expected. These *partner coaches* can be selected before class begins, and they do not have to have their own work done to assist.

# Giving Students Choices to Enhance Learning

Allow for student choice whenever possible. Students usually know how they learn best, and if you can offer them a variety of ways in which to show you that they know the material, they will feel more successful and will be more invested in the work. Examples of ways choice can be incorporated into your classroom include

- Choosing a homework assignment from three that are acceptable
- Choosing a partner to work with on a project
- Choosing an independent reading book
- Choosing the type of test (multiple choice, essay, short answer)
- Creating a test by choosing all the items that would go on the test

List other ways to incorporate choice into your classroom that would promote student interest:

_____

_____

_____

Here is an example of how choice of strategy could be used to meet an objective. To solve a particular work problem, students could choose to

- Use paper and pencil
- Use manipulatives
- Draw the answer
- Work alone
- Work with a partner
- Act out the answer

Can you think of ways in which you could provide your students with choices without disrupting the curriculum and while supporting the needs of diverse learners?

_____

_____

_____

February

# Homework and Opportunities for Enrichment

### Enrichment

Enrichment can be offered to students who have a deeper interest in the topic or to those who may complete class work early (and accurately). Special activities in a learning center, questions on the board, or enrichment sheets provide opportunities for more connection to a particular topic.

Discuss enrichment activities for gifted and talented students, students who complete work early, or students who have a genuine interest in this topic.

Ideas for enrichment:

_____

_____

*Note:* Enrichment should not just be a reward for those who complete their work early. Students who work at varying paces may never have a chance to try more challenging activities offered. Create one day a month as *enrichment* day and let students select a topic they truly enjoy learning about. These topics could become "clubs," where students meet regularly to learn more about what they like.

### Homework

Discuss homework policies. Do students have to pass in homework? Is it always required? Does it only relate to the text? Do students get to select homework activities? Is homework extra credit? Does your mentor teacher correct homework? If not, how does it count toward the grade? Is there such a thing as *creative homework?*

What happens if students don't do their homework? For example, students are assigned a chapter to read in a book and you designed a lesson around the expectation that they had read it. What do you do about the planned lesson?

From Pelletier, Carol Marra. *Strategies For Successful Student Teaching: A Comprehensive Guide,* 2/e. Published by Allyn and Bacon, Boston, MA. Copyright © 2004 by Pearson Education. Reprinted by permission of the publisher.

# How Much Time?

How much time are you spending on different parts of your lessons? Do you spend enough time trying to engage the learners with the content? Are you using active inquiry approaches to engage learners?

**Sample**

| Topic | Time Starts | Time Ends | Total |
|---|---|---|---|
| Introduction to lesson | _____ | _____ | _____ |
| Giving directions | _____ | _____ | _____ |
| Lecturing | _____ | _____ | _____ |
| Answering questions | _____ | _____ | _____ |
| Asking questions | _____ | _____ | _____ |
| Practice work | _____ | _____ | _____ |
| Reprimanding | _____ | _____ | _____ |
| Checking for understanding | _____ | _____ | _____ |
| Students actively engaged/ demonstrating learning | _____ | _____ | _____ |

What took up the most time during the lesson?

_____

_____

_____

_____

What took up the least time during the lesson?

_____

_____

_____

_____

February

# Classroom and Behavior Management Issues

Reward your students for good behavior. The key to rewards is finding out what students really value. Each grade level is very different. Ask your mentor and other new teachers to share what they think would be valuable to the students in your classes.  Ask your students what they value.

Here are some typical rewards for elementary and secondary students. What would you add? What would you never use? Why?

| *Elementary Rewards* | *Secondary Rewards* |
|---|---|
| Free time | Free time |
| Watch a video | Read a magazine |
| Do errands for the teacher | Work on computer |
| Lead the line | See a film/video |
| Go to the reading center | Food |
| Pick out a book | Class trip |
| Play with the pet in class | Play sports during day |
| Listen to music in class | Listen to CD in class |
| Stickers | Wear a hat in class |
| Pencils | Use the video camera |
| Ice cream | Time off from school |
| A certificate | Be coach's assistant |
| Pizza party | Make a t-shirt |
| Magic markers | Teach a class |
| Free recess | Free homework pass |
| Sit next to a friend for a day | Read a newspaper |

## Looking at Student Work

### What Should the Student Learn Next?

Review samples of student work that is below standard. When students have so many skills below standard it can be overwhelming to you as a teacher. Approach this systematically and find *one* skill that would be the next thing this student should learn. Take underperforming learners and move them, step by step, toward standards that allow the student to feel some level of success. This activity also allows you to focus on one skill and identify it clearly. What should the student learn next that is developmentally appropriate for that student?

| Student | Skills the Student Is Not Meeting | One Skill the Student Could Focus on Next to Improve Learning |
|---|---|---|
| 1. | | |
| 2. | | |
| 3. | | |
| 4. | | |

Notice and discuss with your mentor any patterns or trends that emerge about what one thing these students need to do next to learn.

February

# Communicating with Parents

### Monthly Content Updates

Discuss simple ways you can share the content you are teaching in your classroom. Parents need to know what the students are learning so, when you contact them, they understand how they can be helpful at home. Parents can also be valuable resources to teaching. Use the Monthly Content Update as a way to get volunteers or donations. One idea is to send home a weekly notice listing what content is being taught. Elementary teachers may use something like the following. Secondary teachers would modify this for one specific subject.

| Content Update for February<br>Mrs. Smith, Grade 5 | | |
|---|---|---|
| **Content Areas** | **What We Are Learning** | **How You Can Help Us Learn** |
| Math | Fractions | Donate some manipulates we can use.<br><br>Come to class as a volunteer to tutor students. |
| Science | Ecology unit (saving our rivers) | Be a guest speaker.<br><br>Allow us to visit you at your work (i.e., field trip). |
| Social studies | World War II | Be a guest speaker (you know about the war or a grandparent may have served in the war). |
| Language arts | Writing letters | Share your letter-writing skills and sample letters you have written.<br><br>Donate stationery, stamps, and pens so the class can write real letters to people in a nursing home. |

Contact Mrs. Smith at 552-XXXX if you can help our class this month! Thank you.

Discuss with your mentor or other new teachers other ways you can let the parents know what you are doing.

From Pelletier, Carol M. *Mentoring In Action: A Month-by-Month Curriculum For Mentors And Their New Teachers*, 1/e. Published by Allyn and Bacon, Boston, MA. Copyright © 2006 by Pearson Education. Reprinted by permission of the publisher.

# Observing Yourself through Active Listening

You can learn a lot about your practice by listening to yourself on audiotape. Find the audio equipment and tapes at school or bring them in. Listen for the level of vocabulary you use during the lesson, your tone, how often you use your voice to reprimand or praise (and what it sounded like), how clear you were, and whether you had to repeat yourself. Ask yourself what your voice sounds like. Was it high or low? Were you speaking too quickly? Was your voice engaging for learners? Sometimes you will hear unexpected surprises on the tape.

1. List two or three things you would like to listen for in the audiotape and write them down.

   *Examples:*  My tone of voice, whether I call on all girls or boys, how I respond to student questions, how I give directions

   _____

   _____

   _____

   _____

   _____

2. Listen to the tape. What did you hear related to the areas listed in question 1?

   _____

   _____

   _____

   _____

   _____

3. After listening to the tape, ask yourself, "If I was a student in this class, would I be engaged in learning?" How would you respond?

   _____

   _____

   _____

   _____

   _____

   _____

February

## Preparing a Professional Portfolio

Collect samples of your work all year. Use a box to begin the process of collection, or a file cabinet. Don't worry about sorting yet. Then, toward the end of the year, look at what you have collected and sort it into categories. Use this page as a guide for the categories and then organize a few of your samples in a professional portfolio. Write a caption or brief description to highlight why this sample was selected. Items you might collect include the following:

____ Samples of student work with their comments

____ Pages from this book related to reflection and goal setting

____ Photographs

____ Video- and audiotapes

____ Excerpts from your journal

____ Sample lesson plans and units

____ Comments from the mentor

____ School activities (meetings, events, etc.)

____ Professional growth (reading, memberships, writing, etc.)

____ Successful classroom management and behavior management systems

____ Other ideas?

Ask other new teachers in your new-teacher support group what they are collecting and why. How can this activity help you plan for year 2?

## ● REFLECTions

**Directions:** Complete as many of the bubble prompts as you would like after you have finished the activities in the chapter and before you set goals. Add your own prompts to blank bubbles if the prompts listed do not meet your needs. Compare and share your reflections with your mentor and other new teachers at a scheduled meeting.

I am still working on . . .

My biggest challenge is . . .

One thing I could do for fun is . . .

My students are . . .

February

## ● SET GOALS Based on Your Needs for Next Month's Reflection and Discussion

**Directions:**

1. Review the pages in this chapter to determine what you need to revisit next month. Use these pages for possible goal ideas. Revisit any of these topics in your new-teacher support group or with your mentor.

2. Use the following to reflect on your anticipated needs. How can your mentor or other new teachers help you?

### Two New-Teacher Needs I Have Right Now!

1. _____

_____

_____

2. _____

_____

_____

### My Mentor Can Assist Me in Meeting These Needs

My mentor can assist me in meeting need 1 by . . . _____

_____

My mentor can assist me in meeting need 2 by . . . _____

_____

### My New-Teacher Support Group Can Assist Me

My support group can assist me in meeting need 1 by . . . _____

_____

My support group can assist me in meeting need 2 by . . . _____

_____

# March

# Collaborating with New Teachers
## Observing and Building a Trusting Relationship

**New-Teacher Phase:** Collegiality

*"I want to improve my practice.
Can you help me?"*

## INTASC Principles

Review INTASC Principle 10 with your mentor.

- **Principle 10 Interpersonal Relationships**
  The teacher fosters relationships with school colleagues, parents, and agencies in the larger community to support students' learning and well-being.

## Collaborating with New Teachers
### Observing and Building a Trusting Relationship

Collaboration can be fun. Teaching has often been called an *isolating profession*, and many people think it is still that way. Today there are more opportunities to team teach, create a curriculum together, work across disciplines, and create teacher study groups. Collaboration is work. It means meetings, discussions, and decisions based on input from more than one person. Some teachers think it just isn't worth it; others have made it enjoyable and refreshing, given the fact they spend most of their day with students. What do you think? Discuss collegiality and professionalism with your mentor and other new teachers with whom you work. What does it mean to them?

The quote from the student on the title page for this month lets you know that students notice when teachers are having fun doing what they are doing. It makes a difference if a teacher presents a lesson that he or she really feels passionate about. What do you like to teach? How do the students know you like it?

INTASC Principle 10 highlights the importance of building relationships beyond school. Think of ways in which you can connect with agencies, parents, and the business community. How will these professional relationships help your students learn?

Review all the pages in this month to determine what you might like to focus on this month. Use all of these process pages as a guide to enrich the quality of your monthly conversations with your mentor and other new teachers.

## ● Journal Entry

**Directions:** Read the cover page and the narrative for this month. How does this month's topic, the quotes, phase, and narrative overview relate to you right now? Are you comfortable with this topic? Do you need some help? How are you feeling right now?

Use your journal to record your thoughts, feelings, and questions in a free-flowing narrative. This page is for your personal reflection; it does not need to be shared as a written document. You are, however, encouraged to share excerpts with other new teachers or with your mentor as needed.

Reflections:

*Today . . .*

Date _____

## ● PLAN Being Mentored . . . In Action!

### *Questions for Participating in a Quality Conversation*

Participating in a mentoring conversation requires you to be fully engaged. It requires listening and being open to what your mentor is sharing. This means you need to think about the questions you have and how to ask them. It does not mean you have to copy exactly what your mentor recommends, but it does mean you will reflect on the conversations and think about what makes sense for you.

Other new teachers have had these questions in March. Check the questions that you would like to discuss with your mentor or other new teachers in the building or district.

#### New Teachers' Possible Questions:

_____ How do I get to know the other teachers in the school?

_____ What are some of the local agencies I should be aware of that can assist me with students or that offer resources for teachers?

_____ I would like to sponsor some kind of parent event in my classroom. Can you help me navigate school politics to do that?

_____ What else do I need to know about relationships in this school that will assist me with my students?

_____ Other questions I have . . .

## ● Be Prepared

### *Your Mentor May Also Ask You Questions!*

#### Mentor's Possible Questions:

_____ How can I help you connect with other new teachers in the school or district?

_____ How are you getting along with other teachers right now?

_____ What is your next step in connecting with parents?

_____ What can I do to assist you right now that would reduce your anxiety?

## ● Monthly Organizer
### *What I Need to Do Each Month*

**Collaborating with New Teachers:**
**Observing and Building a Trusting Relationship**

| *Pages in this month's chapter help me to . . .* | | |
|---|---|---|
| **PLAN** | Read the title page quotes and standards | page 177 |
| | Read the narrative page | page 178 |
| | Read "Plan Your Time Wisely" | page 182 |
| | Complete the calendar with meeting dates | page 183 |
| **CONNECT** | Review connections | page 184 |
| | Connect with other new teachers | page 184 |
| **ACT** | Review the list of choices | page 185 |
| | Complete the pages you selected | pages 188–198 |
| **REFLECT** | Complete your journal entry | page 179 |
| | Fill in the bubbles | page 199 |
| **SET GOALS** | What's next for you? | page 200 |

March

## ● PLAN Your Time Wisely

### What Is Important to You?

As a new teacher, you will quickly discover you don't seem to have enough time to do it all! Planning your time wisely is crucial to your success in the classroom. Schedule meetings with your mentor and other new teachers early, and put the dates and times in your planning calendar. Make these meetings a priority each month.

- Meetings with your mentor or colleagues may be held before, during, or after school.

- Schedule personal quiet time for yourself to reflect and write in this guide so you can capture your feelings, ideas, and modifications for teaching each month. You can't remember everything, and writing in this guide will document your practice so you can use this as a guide during your second year of teaching.

- Schedule time to read the pages in this guidebook that relate to you. Skim the entire book so you are familiar with the topics. It is OK to skip around or read all the classroom management pages first! Use the monthly topics as a guide for group discussions with other new or experienced teachers, or with your mentor.

### Location and Time for Meetings

Use the key at the bottom of the calendar page to indicate the time of your meeting and place it on the calendar along with the time, length of meeting, and location. Select a private location for meetings with your mentor or colleagues. Make sure you select a place where you will not be interrupted. Meetings may range from five minutes to an hour! What works for you will depend on what you need and what the focus of the meeting is for that day.

What else could you include on your calendar to keep yourself organized?

- Faculty meetings
- Parent conferences
- Professional development workshops

> **What Do I Need to Be Successful Right Now?**

# March Calendar

| MONDAY | TUESDAY | WEDNESDAY | THURSDAY | FRIDAY |
|--------|---------|-----------|----------|--------|
|        |         |           |          |        |
|        |         |           |          |        |
|        |         |           |          |        |
|        |         |           |          |        |
|        |         |           |          |        |

March

Key: B = Before school   D = During the day (preparation time or lunchtime)   A = After school

## ● CONNECT with People, Readings, Professional Associations, Resources, and Technology

▶ *What are the resources that exist in your school and community that could assist you in collaborating with others?*

**Directions:**

1. Review your journal entry and questions from the *PLAN Being Mentored . . . In Action!* page for this month.

2. How can you *connect* with people in your school or district, readings, professional associations, resources, or technology to help you? You may complete this page by yourself, with your mentor, or with a group of new teachers.

### CONNECT *with People . . .*

Who in the school building (experienced teachers, other beginning teachers, custodians, secretaries, etc.) may be able to help with March needs?

What agencies in the community should be used as collaborating partners?

How can parents be helpful this month?

**Names:**

### CONNECT *with Readings, Professional Associations, and Resources . . .*

What have you read or used that would assist in networking with other adults? You may refer to student teaching courses and readings. Your mentor may have books that relate to this topic.

**Titles:**

### CONNECT *with Technology . . .*

Find websites and links that will provide information about

- Teacher collaboration
- Teacher leadership
- Collaborating with parents and other community agencies
- The role of business partners in schools
- Teachers teaching teachers
- New teacher support networks

**Websites:**

## ● ACTIVITIES: Select Topics for Reflection and Discussion
### *What Should I Be Thinking about in March?*

This list of activities requires you to ACT either by reflecting on a topic or discussing the topic with your mentor, other experienced teachers, or other new teachers. These activities are designed to stimulate your thinking. You do not have to complete all of them! Write in this book so you will have documentation of your thoughts and ideas for next year's planning.

### Collaborating with New Teachers: Observing and Building a Trusting Relationship

| | **FIRST STEP:** Start the month with a new-teacher support group meeting! | |
|:---:|:---|:---:|
| ✓ | **Check the ACTivities from the following list that are most meaningful for you to discuss** | **Page** |
| | ACT 1     Receiving Feedback | 188 |
| | ACT 2     Preconference Conversation Is a Must | 189 |
| | ACT 3     Being Observed | 190 |
| | ACT 4     Preparing for a Principal Observation | 191 |
| | ACT 5     Connecting New Teachers to Professional Organizations | 192 |
| | ACT 6     Connecting to Community Resources | 193 |
| | ACT 7     Classroom and Behavior Management Issues | 194 |
| | ACT 8     Looking at Student Work | 195 |
| | ACT 9     Communicating with Parents | 196 |
| | ACT 10     Being Observed by Your Mentor | 197 |
| | ACT 11     Preparing a Professional Portfolio | 198 |

March

## ● FIRST STEP:  Host a New-Teacher Support Group Meeting

*Have snacks and water or soft drinks available. Hold the meeting in one of your classrooms so you can see teacher ideas in action. Rotate the classroom so you all have a chance to show and tell what you are doing. The host teacher could lead the meeting. Put a colorful sign on your door that says "New-Teacher Meeting. Please do not disturb." You may also want to invite other experienced teachers in the building or district who are also interested in sharing ideas. Set ground rules so everyone has a chance to talk. Use this monthly topic as a guide to keep you focused. Assign a timekeeper and set the next meeting date!*

**First:** Welcome and introduce everyone. Take some time to go around the room and quickly share your name and grade level and one thing that is going really well!

**Then:** Review your February new-teacher REFLECTion bubbles from this guide. If you haven't completed the bubbles, do it now, then discuss what you wrote and how you can help each other.

**Next:** Review the SET GOALS page that you completed after the February support group meeting. How will you meet these goals?

**Begin:** Discuss one or more topics from the ACTivities pages for this month. Which topic do most of you need to discuss right now?

**Network:** Complete the CONNECTion page together.

**Acknowledge:** Recognize what you have done so far this year, and instead of focusing on what you don't know, acknowledge your successes! Remind the group to complete the REFLECTion and SET GOALS pages on their own. The last day of the month is a good time to reflect.

**Share:** End the session with compliments for each other and at least one practical idea for March. Take time to complete the Notes page and set a date for next month's sharing group.

### Notes

Something I learned in the group today . . .

Something I will use in my classroom from this meeting . . .

Questions I have to . . .

    Ask my mentor . . .

    Ask other new teachers . . .

    Ask administrators . . .

Idea to share at the next meeting . . .

March

## Receiving Feedback

As a new teacher you will want to know how you are doing. You might be hard on yourself because you think that you should be able to walk into a classroom and just teach, and you are discovering that it isn't as easy as you may have thought. You probably do want some praise, but you will most likely be looking for some specific feedback from your mentor. You may not even know what you are doing right because you often see the wrong in what you are doing. Sometimes mentors offer suggestions that work in their classrooms, but they may not work in yours or be your style. Receiving feedback is a delicate issue. If your mentor is expecting you to try everything she offers and you don't, she may stop giving feedback or suggestions.

Think about what types of feedback are useful to you. Do you like written feedback so you can think about it later? Do you prefer to have an informal conversation or a formal sit-down meeting? Your reflections will provide you with a lens through which to understand how you can best work with your mentor. The key is to talk about this with your mentor. A good mentor understands what is needed and wanted, but she also can't read your mind. Share your ideas in a way that she can hear them.

| A Sample of Ways a Mentor May Provide Feedback to You: Which Do You Prefer? | | | |
|---|---|---|---|
| | **Verbal** | **Written** | **Other** |
| Informal, unplanned | • Talking after a lesson<br>• Seeing each other in the hallway<br>• A five-minute compliment meeting (see *Mentoring in Action*) | A written note put into the new teacher's mailbox | Introducing the new teachers in the school newspaper |
| Informal, planned | • Any meetings from the appendix for 10, 15, 20, or 30 minutes (see *Mentoring in Action*) | A dialogue journal that the mentor and the new teacher keep | Audiotaping for the new teacher and listening together |
| Formal, planned | • The "first meeting" of the month (see *Mentoring in Action*) | Data collected at formal observations (see next pages) | Videotaping a lesson for the new teacher and discussing it |

# Preconference Conversation Is a Must

If your mentor has the opportunity to observe you in your classroom, ask him to review the protocol he will be using so you know what to expect. If he is using the *Mentoring in Action* book as a guide, read the appropriate page in that book together and decide how the observation will be conducted.

1. Discuss observation techniques* and mutually agree on one you would like your mentor to use to observe you. Your mentor may be a novice observer, so be patient.

2. Discuss the specific purpose of the observation (e.g., to listen for questions, to look at movement, to videotape and look for facial expressions). The more specific you are, the better. The two of you can decide which technique may be suited to the lesson and what particular aspect you might be interested in learning more about.

3. Share your lesson plan and any aspects of the lesson procedure with your mentor at this time. This may include fears or anxieties about presenting the lesson.

4. Set up a time to have the postconference to review the data collected. List the date here and on your planning calendar at the beginning of this chapter.

5. Decide what you will do with the data after they have been collected and reviewed.

*The observation techniques on the next page will guide you and your mentor.

March

## Being Observed

Your mentor may use any of the techniques on this page to collect data about what you are doing and how the students are responding. After the data are collected, sit together and discuss one specific thing that would forward your practice and your students' learning. Acknowledge what is going well and set a date to check in on your progress.

- *Scripting.* Write everything you say or do during the lesson. This is a profile of the lesson in narrative form.


- *Verbal feedback.* Listen to your speaking voice as it relates to asking questions, giving praise, talk time, reprimanding, or gender.


- *Movement.* Record how you move around the room, how students interact with you, or both.


- *Timing.* Record the time it takes for an introduction, giving directions, answering questions, doing assignments, and cleaning up.


- *Audiotaping.* Listen for voice, articulation, directions, or any specific aspect of speech.


- *Videotaping.* Record a lesson and observe it together.

# Preparing for a Principal Observation

You most likely will have had the principal (department chair, assistant principal, or other administrator) in your room before March, but usually in March is when decisions have to be made about rehiring. This evaluation may have more weight on the decision, because principals want to see how the teacher has grown to this point. Your mentor should not be involved in the evaluation process; however, she can be a coach for you in providing you with some tips for success. Here are some ideas you may discuss with your mentor or other new teachers.

### Before the Observation

- Remember the purpose of the principal's observation is to assess, not to criticize. You can learn a lot about yourself as a teacher from outsider observation.
- Write the objective of the lesson on the board and how it relates to school standards. What will the students be learning in this lesson and why are they learning this?
- Talk to other new teachers who have been observed to determine the format of the observation so you can be prepared.
- Meet with the administrator in advance to share the lesson plan and find out what is expected during the observation.
- Plan the lesson completely, with all materials and supplies in place.
- Organize and clean the classroom so the principal can walk around to students' desks.
- Make a list of possible things that could go wrong and discuss them with other new teachers or your mentor so you can prepare.

### During the Observation

- Be yourself and forget the principal is in the room (if you can!).
- Remember you are not perfect and you are willing to learn from feedback during the postconference.

### After the Observation

- Write down your thoughts about how the lesson went and what you think you could do better.
- Set up a postconference meeting with the principal.
- Listen to the feedback and share your perspective.
- Don't defend your actions; rather, be open to suggestions and new learning.
- After the meeting, write in your journal what you learned about yourself during this process.

March

## Connecting New Teachers to Professional Organizations

There are many organizations for teachers today, with focuses ranging from early childhood to secondary subjects. These organizations have local, state, and national conferences and workshops. Most have a professional journal that keeps you updated on current research and practice. Check with your school librarian to determine which organizations the school may already be a member of and which journals are in the library for your use. Share this information at one of your meetings.

### Some Professional Organizations

Association for Supervision and Curriculum Development    www.ascd.org

International Reading Association    www.reading.org

National Association for Early Childhood Educators    www.naecte.org

National Council for the Social Studies    www.ncss.org

National Council of Teachers of English    www.ncte.org

National Council of Teachers of Mathematics    www.nctm.org

National Science Teachers Association    www.nsta.org

In addition, a weekly educational newspaper called *Education Week* (www.edweek.org) highlights national and state news related to education issues.

A variety of teacher magazines also provide practical tips, teacher talk columns, units, lesson plans, and hands-on ideas. Check with your local school library for details.

Which journals, organizations, or magazines appeal to you? _____

### Professional Teachers' Unions

The two large general professional organizations are the National Education Association (NEA) and the American Federation of Teachers (AFT). The NEA was formed to promote professional development and improve teaching practices through collective bargaining. The AFT functions primarily as a labor union to raise salaries and improve working conditions. Your school district may be associated with either the NEA or the AFT through its state affiliate. Talk with the union members in your school to find out more about the professional opportunities available through the teachers associations.

What are the benefits for teacher members? _____

# Connecting to Community Resources

Experienced teachers have found places in the community that give free paper to teachers or groups that come into classrooms to be guest speakers. Ask your mentor to share these resources with you. You shouldn't have to wait for years to find these valuable connections.

*Who are the people in the community you should know?*
- Newspaper editor?
- Reporter?
- Fire Chief?
- Chamber of Commerce President?

*What are the public agencies that could provide support?*
- Public library?
- YMCA?
- Police programs for public safety talks?
- Elder agencies for reading tutors?

*What are the businesses that have supported public education?*
- Food donations for snacks for students?
- Supplies for classrooms?

*What other resources does your mentor know about that can assist you?*

March

# Classroom and Behavior Management Issues

### Individual Conference Reports

If you are having difficulty with a student, meet with that student privately to discuss the issue. Use a conference report like the one on this page to document the conversation and to let the student know that this is a formal meeting. Speaking to misbehaving students in front of their peers and continually reprimanding them probably is not working if you are still doing it in March. The conference report provides documentation if further action is required by you.

---

### Conference Report

Student's Name: _____   Date: _____

Reason for Conference: _____

Summary of Conference: _____

_____

_____

_____

_____

_____

_____

_____

Signature of Teacher: _____

Signature of Student: _____

---

# Looking at Student Work

### What Should You Do Next?

Use the same work samples from February and review the completed table.
Complete the new column to move this student to the next level of performance.

| Student | Skills the Student Is Not Meeting | One Skill the Student Could Focus on Next to Improve Learning | What Do You Need to Do to Move the Student to the *Next Level* of Learning? |
|---|---|---|---|
| 1. | See February | See February | |
| 2. | See February | See February | |
| 3. | See February | See February | |
| 4. | See February | See February | |

Discuss any patterns or trends that emerge during the new-teachers support group
meeting about what needs to be done next with each of these students.

March

# Communicating with Parents

### Collaborating with Adults to Enhance Student Progress

There are a variety of ways in which you can collaborate with parents and other adults in the community to assist them in helping their students make progress. Find out whether the school or district has a formal tutoring program for this type of collaboration. Here are some ideas you could do on your own in addition to or instead of district programs.

### *Parent Workshop and Lecture Nights*

Find out if anyone has ever done this at the school. Usually, several teachers at a school organize a workshop around a topic such as math or reading. Secondary teachers may have a guest speaker talk about a specific topic. The purpose of the event is for the parents to learn the content so they can either help their children at home or just have a better understanding of what their children are learning in school. Students come to the event with their parents and do the workshop together. So an elementary math night would allow the students and their parents to learn about fractions together. The students get to show off a bit, too! A secondary history lecture about World War II would be a professional activity the parents and students could hear together.

### *Business Partnerships*

In some school districts, there are formal business partners who come into the school and tutor students or read to them every Friday. You could find a business sponsor and use the adults in the community as resources to help students in their classrooms. This is a win–win situation for the community and the students. The partnerships could also provide guest speakers and resources. Many businesses update equipment and paper supplies, and would love to donate to a school.

### *Alumni Mentoring Program*

Graduates of local high schools often like to come back to mentor students at risk. If they successfully completed a college program and have a successful life, these students want to share it. Create a way for you to tap into the graduates of the district and assist in matching them with at-risk students in elementary and secondary classrooms. Graduating from high school is important today, and the dropout rate is growing because of failure on high-stakes tests. Mentoring may help, and it can begin early.

# Being Observed by Your Mentor

If your mentor is fortunate enough to have release time to observe you, you may find the feedback form on this page useful. A preconference and a postconference will also provide structure to your mentor's comments. Remember, feedback is just that; it does not mean that you have to accept it or use it. Don't take it personally, and use what you can. Your mentor is there to help.

---

### Feedback Form

Date: _____

Subject/Grade: _____

Title of Lesson: _____

1. How well was the lesson plan written? Was it clear and easy to follow? Did it have a purpose that related to student learning?

2. How well did the new teacher carry out the lesson plan's objectives?

3. Describe one positive aspect of the lesson that demonstrates the new teacher's skills as a beginning teacher.

4. How were the students engaged during the lesson to encourage learning?

*Commendations* (positive aspects of teaching demonstrated):

*Recommendations* (suggestions for future lessons):

*Other comments:*

---

March

# Preparing a Professional Portfolio

In January you were invited to describe your teaching qualities. Do the process again and compare your answers with that original process. Use your answers as the basis for a one-page philosophy statement that can be included in your professional portfolio. Take photographs of your classroom. Obtain appropriate permissions for student photos.

1. How have your descriptive words of yourself changed? New words you would use to describe yourself:

   _____, _____, _____

2. How have your beliefs changed? New beliefs you now hold about teaching and learning:

   _____

   _____

   _____

3. List as many concrete examples as you can that relate to the description and beliefs you have written:

   _____

   _____

   _____

After you have compared your philosophy statements and added any new words, use these ideas to write a one-page philosophy statement for the front page of your portfolio. This statement will be the foundation of your portfolio. All artifacts and examples will stem from this platform statement. Remember that your statement should be unique, and should represent who you are as a teacher and how you see yourself.

## ● REFLECTions

**Directions:** Complete as many of the bubble prompts as you like after you have finished the activities in the chapter and before you set goals. Add your own prompts to blank bubbles if the prompts listed do not meet your needs. Compare and share your reflections with your mentor and other new teachers at a scheduled meeting.

The best thing that happened this month is . . .

The thing that has helped me the most this year is . . .

Something I would like to see my mentor teach is . . .

I would like to _____ with my mentor.

March

## ● SET GOALS Based on Your Needs for Next Month's Reflection and Discussion

**Directions:**

1. Review the pages in this chapter to determine what you need to revisit next month. Use these pages for possible goal ideas. Revisit any of these topics in your new-teacher support group or with your mentor.

2. Use the following to reflect on your anticipated needs. How can your mentor or other new teachers help you?

---

### Two New-Teacher Needs I Have Right Now!

1. _____

_____

_____

2. _____

_____

_____

### My Mentor Can Assist Me in Meeting These Needs

My mentor can assist me in meeting need 1 by . . . _____

_____

My mentor can assist me in meeting need 2 by . . . _____

_____

### My New-Teacher Support Group Can Assist Me

My support group can assist me in meeting need 1 by . . . _____

_____

My support group can assist me in meeting need 2 by . . . _____

_____

*A good teacher goes to teacher school.* —First-Grade Student

# Standards
## Creating Meaningful Standards-Based Learning Experiences for Students

**New-Teacher Phase:** Confusion

*"How can I teach what is important and also meet the district standards for high-stakes tests?"*

## INTASC Principles

Revisit INTASC Principles 1 through 7 with your mentor.

- **Principle 1  Making Content Meaningful** (see October)
- **Principle 2  Child Development and Learning Theory** (see September)
- **Principle 3  Learning Styles/Diversity** (see November)
- **Principle 4  Instructional Strategies/Problem Solving** (see December)
- **Principle 5  Motivation and Behavior** (see September)
- **Principle 6  Communication/Knowledge** (see February)
- **Principle 7  Planning for Instruction** (see October)

## Standards

### Creating Meaningful Standards-Based Learning Experiences for Students

The first-grade student who said, "A good teacher goes to teacher school" really knew something. You may have attended teacher preparation school in a school of education or you might be in an alternative program that will endorse you as a teacher. Knowing how to teach makes a difference! Just because you know the content doesn't mean you can teach it to students. Your mentor may be working with new teachers who were prepared (or not) to become teachers. Even if you completed student teaching, it doesn't mean you can teach alone in your own classroom. Adding standards to your already overwhelming work could be really stressful. Take it one step at a time.

If you were prepared to teach "one way" in schools of education that focused on student learning, and now you are told the students must pass high-stakes district or state tests at all costs, you may feel caught in the middle of a philosophical discussion. How can you do both? Do you have to teach to the state test to meet the passing rates? What should you do? Every district and school is wrestling with this dilemma. Of course, proponents of the tests say just teach the way you teach and the students will pass. Discuss this issue with other new teachers and your mentor.

Use all the pages this month as a guide to enrich the quality of your monthly mentoring conversations.

## ● Journal Entry

**Directions:** Read the cover page and the narrative for this month. How does this month's topic, the quotes, phase, and narrative overview relate to you right now? Are you comfortable with this topic? Do you need some help? How are you feeling right now?

Use your journal to record your thoughts, feelings, and questions in a free-flowing narrative. This page is for your personal reflection; it does not need to be shared as a written document. You are, however, encouraged to share excerpts with other new teachers or with your mentor as needed.

### Reflections:

*Today . . .*

Date _____

April

## ● PLAN Being Mentored . . . In Action!

### *Questions for Participating in a Quality Conversation*

Participating in a mentoring conversation requires you to be fully engaged. It requires listening and being open to what your mentor is sharing. This means you need to think about the questions you have and how to ask them. It does not mean you have to copy exactly what your mentor recommends, but it does mean you will reflect on the conversations and think about what makes sense for you.

Other new teachers have had these questions in April. Check the questions that you would like to discuss with your mentor or other new teachers in your school or district.

### New Teachers' Possible Questions:

_____ Can you review with me how to make content meaningful?

_____ My students seem to be changing at this time of year. I need help remembering my adolescent and child psychology. Is this supposed to be happening, or are my students different?

_____ The diversity in my room is overwhelming. I have so many learning styles. What can I do?

_____ Instructional strategies for diverse learners are important, but I find myself teaching the whole class the same way. Do you have any suggestions?

_____ The behavior in my room is really challenging. I need a refresher. Are there any support systems for me right now?

_____ I am trying to communicate in different ways with my students. Can you review them with me to be sure I am on track?

_____ I don't have time to plan the way I did in the fall. I know that when I do, the day goes much better, but I just can't fit everything in. Can you help me get organized?

_____ Other questions I have . . .

## ● Be Prepared

### *Your Mentor May Also Ask You Questions!*

### Mentor's Possible Question:

_____ What can I do to assist you right now that would reduce your anxiety?

## ● Monthly Organizer

*What I Need to Do Each Month*

**Standards:**
**Creating Meaningful Standards-Based**
**Learning Experiences for Students**

April

## ● PLAN Your Time Wisely

### What Is Important to You?

As a new teacher, you will quickly discover you don't seem to have enough time to do it all! Planning your time wisely is crucial to your success in the classroom. Schedule meetings with your mentor and other new teachers early, and put the dates and times in your planning calendar. Make these meetings a priority each month.

- Meetings with your mentor or colleagues may be held before, during, or after school.

- Schedule personal quiet time for yourself to reflect and write in this guide so you can capture your feelings, ideas, and modifications for teaching each month. You can't remember everything, and writing in this guide will document your practice so you can use this as a guide during your second year of teaching.

- Schedule time to read the pages in this guidebook that relate to you. Skim the entire book so you are familiar with the topics. It is OK to skip around or read all the classroom management pages first! Use the monthly topics as a guide for group discussions with other new or experienced teachers, or with your mentor.

### Location and Time for Meetings

Use the key at the bottom of the calendar page to indicate the time of your meeting and place it on the calendar along with the time, length of meeting, and location. Select a private location for meetings with your mentor or colleagues. Make sure you select a place where you will not be interrupted. Meetings may range from five minutes to an hour! What works for you will depend on what you need and what the focus of the meeting is for that day.

What else could you include on your calendar to keep yourself organized?

- Faculty meetings
- Parent conferences
- Professional development workshops

### What Do I Need to Be Successful Right Now?

# April Calendar

| MONDAY | TUESDAY | WEDNESDAY | THURSDAY | FRIDAY |
|--------|---------|-----------|----------|--------|
|  |  |  |  |  |
|  |  |  |  |  |
|  |  |  |  |  |
|  |  |  |  |  |
|  |  |  |  |  |

Key: B = Before school  D = During the day (preparation time or lunchtime)  A = After school

## ● CONNECT with People, Readings, Professional Associations, Resources, and Technology

▶ *What are the resources that exist in your school and community that could assist you in creating meaningful standards-based learning experiences?*

**Directions:**

1. Review your journal entry and questions from the *PLAN Being Mentored . . . In Action!* page for this month.

2. How can you *connect* with people in your school or district, readings, professional associations, resources, or technology to help you? You may complete this page by yourself, with your mentor, or with a group of new teachers.

### CONNECT *with People . . .*

Who in the school building (experienced teachers, other beginning teachers, custodians, secretaries, etc.) may be able to help with April needs?

What district departments relate to testing and curriculum?

How can parents be helpful in assisting around curriculum and testing issues?

**Names:**

### CONNECT *with Readings, Professional Associations, and Resources . . .*

What have you read or used that would assist you in learning more about curricula, testing, and standards? You may refer to student teaching courses and readings. Your mentor may have books or district documents that relate to this topic.

**Titles:**

### CONNECT *with Technology . . .*

Find websites and links that will provide information about

- All INTASC Principles
- State and local standards
- District curriculum frameworks
- Testing policies and mandates
- No Child Left Behind Act

**Websites:**

## ● ACTIVITIES: Select Topics for Reflection and Discussion
### *What Should I Be Thinking about in April?*

This list of activities requires you to ACT either by reflecting on a topic or discussing the topic with your mentor, other experienced teachers, or other new teachers. These activities are designed to stimulate your thinking. You do not have to complete all of them! Write in this book so you will have documentation of your thoughts and ideas for next year's planning.

## Standards:
## Creating Meaningful Standards-Based Learning Experiences for Students

| | FIRST STEP:   Start the month with a new-teacher support group meeting! | | |
|:---:|---|---|:---:|
| ✓ | **Check the ACTivities from the following list that are most meaningful for you to discuss** | | **Page** |
| | ACT 1 | Relating Classroom Curriculum to District Standards | 212 |
| | ACT 2 | Teacher Talking Time versus Student Talking Time | 213 |
| | ACT 3 | Relating Standards to Real Life | 214 |
| | ACT 4 | Observing an Individual Student | 215 |
| | ACT 5 | Observing a Small Group | 216 |
| | ACT 6 | Classroom and Behavior Management Issues | 217 |
| | ACT 7 | Looking at Student Work | 218 |
| | ACT 8 | Communicating with Parents | 219 |
| | ACT 9 | Being Observed | 220 |
| | ACT 10 | Preparing a Professional Portfolio | 221 |
| | ACT 11 | New-Teacher Needs | 222 |

April

## ● FIRST STEP:  Host a New-Teacher Support Group Meeting

*Have snacks and water or soft drinks available. Hold the meeting in one of your classrooms so you can see teacher ideas in action. Rotate the classroom so you all have a chance to show and tell what you are doing. The host teacher could lead the meeting. Put a colorful sign on your door that says "New-Teacher Meeting. Please do not disturb." You may also want to invite other experienced teachers in the building or district who are also interested in sharing ideas. Set ground rules so everyone has a chance to talk. Use this monthly topic as a guide to keep you focused. Assign a timekeeper and set the next meeting date!*

**First:** Welcome and introduce everyone. Take some time to go around the room and quickly share your name and grade level, and one thing that is going really well!

**Then:** Review your March new-teacher REFLECTion bubbles from this guide. If you haven't completed the bubbles, do it now, then discuss what you wrote and how you can help each other.

**Next:** Review the SET GOALS page that you completed after the March support group meeting. How will you meet these goals?

**Begin:** Discuss one or more topics from the ACTivities pages for this month. Which topic do most of you need to discuss right now?

**Network:** Complete the CONNECTion page together.

**Acknowledge:** Recognize what you have done so far this year and, instead of focusing on what you don't know, acknowledge your successes! Remind the group to complete the REFLECTion and SET GOALS pages on their own. The last day of the month is a good time to reflect.

**Share:** End the session with compliments for each other and at least one practical idea for April. Take time to complete the Notes page and set a date for next month's sharing group.

## *Notes*

Something I learned in the group today . . .

Something I will use in my classroom from this meeting . . .

Questions I have to . . .

    Ask my mentor . . .

    Ask other new teachers . . .

    Ask administrators . . .

Idea to share at the next meeting . . .

April

# Relating Classroom Curriculum to District Standards

Think about the word *standards* and how they are being actualized in your classroom. Ask your mentor to talk to you about them. Do you have examples of standards-based lessons to share? Use the following questions as a guide for your discussions in your new-teacher support group or with your mentor. Remember that standards are not activities. As a new teacher you may get excited about doing activities with your students, but then you may have difficulty relating what you are doing to a required district standard.

### Lesson Plan Discussion

This process can be done prior to teaching a lesson or after a lesson has been taught so you can reflect and make changes to future lesson plans.

1. What is the purpose of this lesson?

2. Why are you teaching this?

3. Why now?

4. Is it part of a larger unit of study?

5. Which district or state standards (curriculum objectives) relate to this lesson?

6. Why did you select them?

7. How do you think students will respond to this lesson?

8. Will all learners be engaged? How will you know?

9. Is there any aspect of your lesson you anticipate may be challenging? Why?

10. What is the most valuable part of this lesson that relates to learning?

11. Other?

# Teacher Talking Time versus Student Talking Time

An excellent soccer coach once said, "A good player is created by giving her as many 'touches on the ball' as possible during every practice session." Teachers who talk the entire lesson and never let the students talk or engage in the curriculum are like coaches who tell the players *how* to do it, but never let them practice *doing* it. Notice how much time you are talking during your lessons (use your taped lesson from a previous month to measure accurately) and how much time you allow the students to talk to each other. Are you planning time in your lessons for your students to talk and to engage in meaningful learning activities? Give your students as many "touches on the ball" as you can in one class.

Review your responses to February ACT 4, How Much Time?, to reflect on what you are doing right now. You use your voice all day long in many different ways. Some of your voice comments relate to learning and others do not. When do student voices get heard in your class?

How can you increase appropriate student talking time?

- Integrate paired sharing into lessons.
- Allow time for discussion in lessons.
- Begin each class with time for students to share what they already know about a topic.
- End a class with time to share what they learned today.
- Partner English language learners with native speakers.
- Include read-aloud activities in lessons.
- Add your ideas here.

Emphasize that student talking needs to relate to learning objectives that relate to the standards. You need to be mindful at all times of what you are teaching and why. Allowing student learners to talk in class is one way to keep them alert and engaged. Just like in soccer, players who are on the field have to be engaged. The students won't be bored and are less likely to misbehave if they are "playing" in the game.

April

## Relating Standards to Real Life

You can use the community to make the standards come alive for your students. Find ways your students can participate in *service learning* in the community that relates to your content area. What can you add to the following list? Take time to recognize which standard you are meeting by doing this work. What are the students supposed to know and be able to do as a result of this service? Ask your mentor to help you relate standards to real life.

Examples of service learning activities include the following:

| | |
|---|---|
| History, middle/high | Interview and audiotape World War II veterans and then have them come to the classroom as guest speakers. Provide a service to the local veteran's association as part of this activity. |
| Science, middle/high | Connect with a recycling center on a project that relates to the science unit on recycling. |
| Elementary | Write to the elderly and visit them on holidays. Do this as part of the language arts curriculum. |
| Elementary, middle, high | Volunteer at a shelter or soup kitchen and write about the experience. |
| Elementary | Invite local businesses to the classroom while learning about professions and select one that needs a special project completed. |

Other ideas?

_____

_____

_____

Why is it important to have students make the connection between learning information and service learning?

# Observing an Individual Student

At this time of year, you will have at least one student who is a challenge. It is easy to blame the student; after all, the student is the one who is acting out. Approach the situation more clinically and less personally as you observe one of your students who is challenging. Use the following form along with your observation skills to delve deeper into this student's world. Think like an ethnographer instead of a teacher. This exercise may bring new evidence to the surface that may assist you in working with this student for the rest of the year. You may need to do this process more than once.

---

### Student Observation

First Name of Student: _____    Date of Observation: _____

Challenge This Student Presents for You:

1. What do you notice about this student (physical appearance, cultural background, language, social interaction, skills and abilities, motivation, attitude, self-concept, etc.)?


2. How does the student respond to your lesson?


3. Does the student interact with any other students? Describe.


4. What is the quality of the student's work?


5. Name something positive the student did during the lesson.


6. What other things did you observe that you didn't know about the student?

---

From Pelletier, Carol Marra. *Strategies For Successful Student Teaching: A Comprehensive Guide*, 2/e. Published by Allyn and Bacon, Boston, MA. Copyright © 2004 by Pearson Education. Reprinted by permission of the publisher.

April

## Observing a Small Group

You are encouraged to group your students to enhance learning; but, often, grouping students creates behavior problems. So what should you do? Not grouping leaves students bored and teachers doing all the talking, yet grouping may be too challenging. Observe a small group in action and see what works and what doesn't.

After you have stepped back and observed a group, use the following questions as a guide and talk with your mentor or other new teachers about creating ground rules for working in groups. All group work should relate to the curriculum standard and should not just be busy work.

1. Why is this small group working together?

2. Who is the leader of the group? Self appointed or teacher appointed?

3. How effective is the leader?

4. Is the group completing the assigned task? How do you know?

5. Are all members of the group participating? What are the differences in the individual members' contributions to the group? Give an example.

6. What is your overall impression of this group activity?

# Classroom and Behavior Management Issues

### Student Contract

At this time of the year, students will be testing your patience and your skills. Sometimes it helps to have students state in writing how they will change their disruptive behavior. Here is a model of a student contract. Invent your own format, too. The key here is to have students write about how their success will be measured. How will you know the student's behavior has changed? Also, the reward is important and you should add "by [date] or else the reward expires." The contract can also be designed for groups by changing *I* to *we*.

---

**Student Contract**

I state that I will (*change a certain behavior*) _____

_____ .

I will measure my success by (*how the behavior will be noted as being done*) _____

_____ .

For successful demonstration (*I will receive a reward*) _____

_____ .

Signed (teacher): _____   Date: _____

Signed (student): _____   Date: _____

---

April

# Looking at Student Work

### What Are the Students Doing Right?

Review a set of papers. Sort them into the following categories and think about the kinds of compliments you can give to acknowledge what a student is learning. Your intention is to focus on what is correct to move the student to the next level of understanding.

| Below Standard | Meets the Standard | Above Standard |
|---|---|---|
| How many papers here? _____ <br><br> % of class _____ <br><br><br> Select *one* paper. What can this student be complimented for? | How many papers here? _____ <br><br> % of class _____ <br><br><br> Select *one* paper. What can this student be complimented for? | How many papers here? _____ <br><br> % of class _____ <br><br><br> Select *one* paper. What can this student be complimented for? |

Think about this process and relate it to your own work and skill level as a new teacher. Do compliments work for you? Discuss with your mentor and other new teachers why complimenting students is important to improving their progress. Remember to be specific about your compliments so students know exactly what they did correctly and can repeat that skill.

# Communicating with Parents

### Teaching Effective Study Skills

Parents know schoolwork, homework, and tests are important, but they often don't know how to help their children learn. These parents come to meetings with teachers and want to help, they just don't know what to tell their children to do. Brainstorm ways you can educate parents about effective study habits. Offer a Parent Information Session during the evening that highlights effective study skills. Actually teach the parents what you are teaching the students.

| Effective Study Skill: What Is It? Describe the Skill. | Elementary Students: What Behavior Would Parents See? | Secondary Students: What Behavior Would Parents See? |
|---|---|---|
| Homework paper | | |
| Studying for a test | | |
| Reading a chapter and taking notes | | |

What should parents know and be able to do to help their children learn? Discuss this with your mentor.

April

## Being Observed

Goal setting is critical to observation. After any observation by your mentor or administrator, ask the observer to set one goal with you that they can follow up on later. What one thing could you do that would change your practice? What would that goal be? Make the goal achievable, observable, and measurable.

| Goal | |
|---|---|
| **Actions**<br><br>What will you do to achieve your goal? | |
| **Evaluation**<br><br>Date for goal review _____<br><br>How will you know if you reach your goal? | |

### Sample Goals

Having interesting introductions to lessons

Culminating a lesson in an orderly way

Moving around the classroom

Pronouncing all the words in a lesson correctly

Managing an effective classroom routine during a lesson

# Preparing a Professional Portfolio

Some time this month, review the artifacts you have been collecting in your box. If you are completing a portfolio for the district, you may review district guidelines now to make sure you are gathering what you need. If you are creating a portfolio for professional sharing, ask your mentor or support group to proofread any written documents. You should select artifacts from your box to include in your portfolio that relate to what you believe about teaching and learning, as well as the district standards. Be sure to include your philosophy statement as the first page. Do the following:

1. Review your philosophy of education and rewrite it if needed.

   What do I have that matches what I believe?

   What do I absolutely want to make sure is in my portfolio?

   What is missing that I need to include?

2. Review district or state standards for portfolio submission.

3. Decide on a format (binder, artist portfolio, Web, etc.).

4. Write the table of contents (based on standards).

5. Continue to collect artifacts (audio and video).

6. Set a deadline for completion.

April

## New-Teacher Needs

What do you need this month?

How can you get support?

List some possible people who can help you.

## ● REFLECTions

**Directions:** Complete as many of the bubble prompts as you like after you have finished the activities in the chapter and before you set goals. Add your own prompts to blank bubbles if the prompts listed do not meet your needs. Compare and share your reflections with your mentor and other new teachers at a scheduled meeting.

I am frustrated by . . .

One thing that would make a difference is . . .

Teaching is . . .

I see myself teaching . . .

April

## ● SET GOALS Based on Your Needs for Next Month's Reflection and Discussion

**Directions:**

1. Review the pages in this chapter to determine what you need to revisit next month. Use these pages for possible goal ideas. Revisit any of these topics in your new-teacher support group or with your mentor.

2. Use the following to reflect on your anticipated needs. How can your mentor or other new teachers help you?

---

### Two New-Teacher Needs I Have Right Now!

1. _____
_____
_____

2. _____
_____
_____

### My Mentor Can Assist Me in Meeting These Needs

My mentor can assist me in meeting need 1 by . . . _____
_____

My mentor can assist me in meeting need 2 by . . . _____
_____

### My New-Teacher Support Group Can Assist Me

My support group can assist me in meeting need 1 by . . . _____
_____

My support group can assist me in meeting need 2 by . . . _____
_____

---

*Good teachers listen to their students and care how their students are doing academically.* —High School Student

# Assessing Students' Progress

## High-Stakes Tests and Teacher Assessment

## New-Teacher Phase:  Hope

*"It looks like my students are passing tests and learning. Maybe I can do this."*

## INTASC Principles

Review INTASC Principle 8.

● **Principle 8  Assessment**
The teacher understands and uses formal and informal assessment strategies to evaluate and ensure the continuous intellectual, social, and physical development of the learner.

## Assessing Students' Progress
### High-Stakes Tests and Teacher Assessment

"Good teachers care about how their students are doing academically," said one high school student. Teachers who are actually trying to help students learn, as opposed to just giving tests, make students engage in learning. Are you the kind of teacher who is focused on student learning?

Stay hopeful. Some of your students are passing the tests you give and it actually looks like they may have learned something this year. You might be thinking: *Perhaps I* can *do this after all.* INTASC Principle 8, Assessment, focuses on both formal and informal assessments. Remember that high-stakes tests are not the only measure of success. ACT 1 in this chapter encourages you to discuss the multiple measures of assessment a teacher needs to use to document progress. Learning is developmental, and all students do not learn the identified curriculum the year it is listed in the syllabus. Some learn it later.

Hope is the quality that highlights the service aspect of teaching. Teachers, both new and experienced, hope for the best for their students. You hope what you are doing makes a difference to your students. Hope is positive and allows you to sustain your energy to create new goals for your students. Keep that hope alive for yourself this month. Review the pages in this chapter now so you can determine what you would like to focus on this month.

## ● Journal Entry

**Directions:** Read the cover page and the narrative for this month. How does this month's topic, the quotes, phase, and narrative overview relate to you right now? Are you comfortable with this topic? Do you need some help? How are you feeling right now?

Use your journal to record your thoughts, feelings, and questions in a free-flowing narrative. This page is for your personal reflection; it does not need to be shared as a written document. You are, however, encouraged to share excerpts with other new teachers or with your mentor as needed.

---

### Reflections:

*Today . . .*

May

Date _____

## ● PLAN Being Mentored . . . In Action!
### *Questions for Participating in a Quality Conversation*

Participating in a mentoring conversation requires you to be fully engaged. It requires listening and being open to what your mentor is sharing. This means you need to think about the questions you have and how to ask them. It does not mean you have to copy exactly what your mentor recommends, but it does mean you will reflect on the conversations and think about what makes sense for you.

Other new teachers have had these questions in May. Check the questions that you would like to discuss with your mentor or other new teachers in your school or district.

### New Teachers' Possible Questions:

_____ How do I grade these students at the end of the year?

_____ High-stakes tests are taking so much time. How do I fit in my teaching?

_____ What end-of-the-year assessments do I need to know?

_____ How do you think I am doing?

_____ Other questions I have . . .

## ● Be Prepared

### *Your Mentor May Also Ask You Questions!*

### Mentor's Possible Questions:

_____ What do you need to do right now?

_____ What paperwork do you need to discuss?

_____ What can I do to assist you right now that would reduce your anxiety?

## ● Monthly Organizer
### *What I Need to Do Each Month*

**Assessing Students' Progress:**
**High-Stakes Tests and Teacher Assessment**

| *Pages in this month's chapter help me to . . .* | | |
|---|---|---|
| **PLAN** | Read the title page quotes and standards | page 225 |
| | Read the narrative page | page 226 |
| | Read "Plan Your Time Wisely" | page 230 |
| | Complete the calendar with meeting dates | page 231 |
| **CONNECT** | Review connections | page 232 |
| | Connect with other new teachers | page 232 |
| **ACT** | Review the list of choices | page 233 |
| | Complete the pages you selected | pages 236–242 |
| **REFLECT** | Complete your journal entry | page 227 |
| | Fill in the bubbles | page 243 |
| **SET GOALS** | What's next for you? | page 244 |

May

## ● PLAN Your Time Wisely

### What Is Important to You?

As a new teacher, you will quickly discover you don't seem to have enough time to do it all! Planning your time wisely is crucial to your success in the classroom. Schedule meetings with your mentor and other new teachers early, and put the dates and times in your planning calendar. Make these meetings a priority each month.

- Meetings with your mentor or colleagues may be held before, during, or after school.
- Schedule personal quiet time for yourself to reflect and write in this guide so you can capture your feelings, ideas, and modifications for teaching each month. You can't remember everything, and writing in this guide will document your practice so you can use this as a guide during your second year of teaching.
- Schedule time to read the pages in this guidebook that relate to you. Skim the entire book so you are familiar with the topics. It is OK to skip around or read all the classroom management pages first! Use the monthly topics as a guide for group discussions with other new or experienced teachers, or with your mentor.

### Location and Time for Meetings

Use the key at the bottom of the calendar page to indicate the time of your meeting and place it on the calendar along with the time, length of meeting, and location. Select a private location for meetings with your mentor or colleagues. Make sure you select a place where you will not be interrupted. Meetings may range from five minutes to an hour! What works for you will depend on what you need and what the focus of the meeting is for that day.

What else could you include on your calendar to keep yourself organized?

- Faculty meetings
- Parent conferences
- Professional development workshops

---

**What Do I Need to Be Successful Right Now?**

# May Calendar

| MONDAY | TUESDAY | WEDNESDAY | THURSDAY | FRIDAY |
|---|---|---|---|---|
| | | | | |
| | | | | |
| | | | | |
| | | | | |
| | | | | |

Key: B = Before school   D = During the day (preparation time or lunchtime)   A = After school

## ● CONNECT with People, Readings, Professional Associations, Resources, and Technology

▶ *What are the resources that exist in your school and community that could assist new teachers assess students' progress?*

**Directions:**

1. Review your journal entry and questions from the *PLAN Being Mentored . . . In Action!* page for this month.

2. How can you *connect* with people in your school or district, readings, professional associations, resources, or technology to help you? You may complete this page by yourself, with your mentor, or with a group of new teachers.

### CONNECT *with People . . .*

Who in the school building (experienced teachers, other beginning teachers, custodians, secretaries, etc.) may be able to help with May needs?

What district departments relate to assessing student progress and referrals for next year?

How are parents included in end-of-the-year student assessments?

**Names:**

### CONNECT *with Readings, Professional Associations, and Resources . . .*

What have you read or used that would assist understanding high-stakes tests and district assessment policies? You may refer to student teaching courses and readings. Your mentor may have district materials that relate to this topic.

**Titles:**

### CONNECT *with Technology . . .*

Find websites and links that will provide information about

- High-stakes tests
- Retaining students
- End-of-the-year assessments and evaluation
- District policies
- Formal and informal assessments

**Websites:**

## ● ACTIVITIES: Select Topics for Reflection and Discussion

### *What Should I Be Thinking about in May?*

This list of activities requires you to ACT either by reflecting on a topic or by discussing the topic with your mentor, other experienced teachers, or other new teachers. These activities are designed to stimulate your thinking. You do not have to complete all of them! Write in this book so you will have documentation of your thoughts and ideas for next year's planning.

## Assessing Students' Progress:
## High-Stakes Tests and Teacher Assessment

| | | FIRST STEP: Start the month with a new-teacher support group meeting! | |
|---|---|---|---|
| ✓ | | Check the ACTivities from the following list that are most meaningful for you to discuss. | Page |
| | ACT 1 | Assessing Students' Progress | 236 |
| | ACT 2 | Classroom and Behavior Management Issues | 237 |
| | ACT 3 | Looking at Student Work | 238 |
| | ACT 4 | Communicating with Parents | 239 |
| | ACT 5 | Self-assessment | 240 |
| | ACT 6 | Preparing a Professional Portfolio | 241 |
| | ACT 7 | New-Teacher Needs | 242 |

May

## ● FIRST STEP:  Host a New-Teacher Support Group Meeting

*Have snacks and water or soft drinks available. Hold the meeting in one of your classrooms so you can see teacher ideas in action. Rotate the classroom so you all have a chance to show and tell what you are doing. The host teacher could lead the meeting. Put a colorful sign on your door that says "New-Teacher Meeting. Please do not disturb." You may also want to invite other experienced teachers in the building or district who are also interested in sharing ideas. Set ground rules so everyone has a chance to talk. Use this monthly topic as a guide to keep you focused. Assign a timekeeper and set the next meeting date!*

**First:** Welcome and introduce everyone. Take some time to go around the room and quickly share your name and grade level, and one thing that is going really well!

**Then:** Review your April new-teacher REFLECTion bubbles from this guide. If you haven't completed the bubbles, do it now, then discuss what you wrote and how you can help each other.

**Next:** Review the SET GOALS page that you completed after the April support group meeting. How will you meet these goals?

**Begin:** Discuss one or more topics from the ACTivities pages for this month. Which topic do most of you need to discuss right now?

**Network:** Complete the CONNECTion page together.

**Acknowledge:** Recognize what you have done so far this year and, instead of focusing on what you don't know, acknowledge your successes! Remind the group to complete the REFLECTion and SET GOALS pages on their own. The last day of the month is a good time to reflect.

**Share:** End the session with compliments for each other and at least one practical idea for May. Take time to complete the Notes page and set a date for next month's sharing group.

## *Notes*

Something I learned in the group today . . .

Something I will use in my classroom from this meeting . . .

Questions I have to . . .

    Ask my mentor . . .

    Ask other new teachers . . .

    Ask administrators . . .

Idea to share at the next meeting . . .

May

## Assessing Students' Progress

Discuss all the ways in which you can assess a students' progress in school. Use the original student profile information collected in September ACT 3 as one way to observe growth and development. Remember to look at *multiple measures* of growth. How many measures can you think of? View each student as a whole learner, not just a test result.

1. Student personal strengths (related to September ACT 3 profile)
   - Ability to speak languages
   - Musical ability
   - Hobbies
   - Other

2. Interpersonal and social interactions
   - With other students in the classroom
   - Leadership qualities

3. Academic achievement
   - On units of study based on teacher-made tests and quizzes (paper and pencil)
   - Project or performance based

4. High-stakes testing results
   - Math
   - Literacy
   - Other content areas

5. Other valuable information related to this student's progress this year

### Discussion

How do high-stakes tests relate to overall student learning?

# Classroom and Behavior Management Issues

As the year comes to a close, sometimes student misbehavior escalates. Everyone is tired and you may have exhausted your ideas. Here are some commonsense tips for closing out the year. Add your own and discuss why each one is important to building a community of learners. You may have tried some of these ideas before, but try them again now if you need to.

1. Focus on positive behavior when it happens.
   - Give verbal praise for specific behavior.
   - Send notes home with students.
   - Make complimentary phone calls to parents about their child.

2. Don't threaten or bribe students to behave.
   - Students may respond for a short term but will not respect you in the long term, because behavior becomes contingent on continuation of the bribe.

3. Take charge of the classroom in a firm but pleasant manner.
   - Use your sense of humor to keep students in line.
   - Communicate your needs honestly to students.
   - Listen to your students' requests and complaints.

4. Give *I* messages to students instead of *you* messages.
   - "*I* am unhappy with the behavior I am seeing," not "*You* are misbehaving again."

5. Use body language and signals to prevent disruptive behavior.
   - Make eye contact with the misbehaving student.
   - Use a frown or other negative facial expression.
   - Walk near the student and lightly tap his or her shoulder.
   - Use your sense of humor.
   - Use a cue to have the students look at you (e.g., lights off, raise hands).

6. Don't use sarcasm, cruel remarks, or words to embarrass students.
   - No ridicule or intimidation allowed!
   - Never touch a student in an abusive way.
   - Confrontation in front of a whole class is not recommended.
   - If the situation becomes confrontational, remove the student and discuss the problem later.

May

# Looking at Student Work

### What Do We Know and Believe about Differentiating Instruction?

Your district probably has workshops on this topic. Some teachers embrace the concept, others are not sure what it means. Others don't believe there should be any differentiation from the standard and that all learners should be treated the same in a same-age-level classroom. What does your mentor believe about differentiating instruction? Philosophies are personal, but district standards and approaches for student learning are public. How can you discuss the intersection of the teacher's personal belief system and the mandate from the district that all students must learn?

1. Discuss differentiation with your mentor and others. What do you think this means?

2. Ask your mentor to share any specific materials or ideas about ways you can differentiate in your classroom.

3. Share ideas in your new-teacher support group meeting. Note the ideas you want to try here.

4. Look at one sample of student work and differentiate the instruction.

| Student Name | Standard Level: Below, Meets, or Above | What Student Needs to Learn Next | How You Could Differentiate Instruction to Assist the Student |
|---|---|---|---|
|  |  |  |  |

# Communicating with Parents

### Student Progress on High-Stakes Tests and Teacher Tests

High-stakes tests are here to stay. In many districts they mean graduation from high school or not. Teacher-made tests are also part of academic progress and they serve as the grading system for report cards and moving to the next grade. Both tests are critical to students. So how can parents help? Assist parents in understanding the difference between high-stakes tests and teacher tests, and how they both affect their children.

Discuss the ways the district lets parents know about high-stakes tests. Ask your mentor to help you clarify the differences in the tests and how they are used to measure student progress. What are the benefits and limitations of paper-and-pencil testing?

| High-Stakes Tests<br>(State or District) | Teacher-Made Tests<br>(Measure of Content Learned in the Classroom) |
|---|---|
| List how they are used and how students benefit from this test. | List how they are used and how students benefit from this test. |

*May*

## Self-assessment

You have been discussing and reflecting on many aspects of new-teacher performance this year. Rate yourself in these categories. Define *excellent* and *good* before you begin. Are there categories that are missing from this table?

Your indicators of excellent progress would be _____.

Your indicators of good progress would be _____.

| Example of New-Teacher Rubric for Instructional Practice | | | | | |
|---|---|---|---|---|---|
| | Excellent Progress | Good Progress | Needs More Development | Needs Assistance | Unsatisfactory |
| Demonstrates creativity and thought in planning | | | | | |
| Uses a variety of teaching strategies and methods to engage learners | | | | | |
| Develops both long-form and short-form lesson plans | | | | | |
| Demonstrates principles and theories of instruction for students in the classroom | | | | | |
| Demonstrates proper sequencing and pacing of lessons | | | | | |
| Develops and modifies curriculum to meet student needs | | | | | |
| Manages the classroom | | | | | |
| Handles difficult situations through problem-solving approaches | | | | | |
| Maintains an organized classroom for student learning | | | | | |
| Disciplines fairly | | | | | |

From Pelletier, Carol Marra. *Strategies For Successful Student Teaching: A Comprehensive Guide*, 2/e. Published by Allyn and Bacon, Boston, MA. Copyright © 2004 by Pearson Education. Reprinted by permission of the publisher.

# Preparing a Professional Portfolio

A portfolio is not a scrapbook. It is a collection of carefully selected artifacts that tell a story. Carefully select artifacts that you can use to demonstrate your effectiveness as a teacher. Reflecting on your practice is a key component to a portfolio.

*Step 1*.  Review all materials you've collected in your box this year. What stands out as interesting, colorful, and meaningful to share with others?

*Step 2*.  Select key items, photos, samples of student work, notes from parents, and so forth, that illustrate "something" you want to share. It could be a standard for teaching, a competency, a skill, or an interest. It could also be related to the INTASC Principles listed on the cover sheet of each month in this book. Less is more!

*Step 3*.  Write a short description or caption for each item selected. Describe what it is and why it is in the portfolio.

*Step 4*.  Write a short reflection for each item and place it below the description or caption. The reflection explains what you learned from teaching this, what you would do differently, or something that was insightful for you that relates to this photo or lesson.

*Step 5*.  Lay the artifact, description, and reflection on a page under a *title* that clearly identifies the message to the reader. If you are organizing your portfolio according to INTASC Principles, perhaps the standard is part of the title.

*Step 6*.  Put all the pages together. Place the philosophy statement at the beginning and write a final statement for the last page. This final statement could include what you learned this year as a first-year teacher, your goals for year 2, and your future aspirations as an educator.

May

## New-Teacher Needs

What do you need this month?

How can you get support?

List some possible people who can help you.

## ● REFLECTions

**Directions:** Complete as many of the bubble prompts as you like after you have finished the activities in the chapter and before you set goals. Add your own prompts to blank bubbles if the prompts listed do not meet your needs. Compare and share your reflections with your mentor and other new teachers at a scheduled meeting.

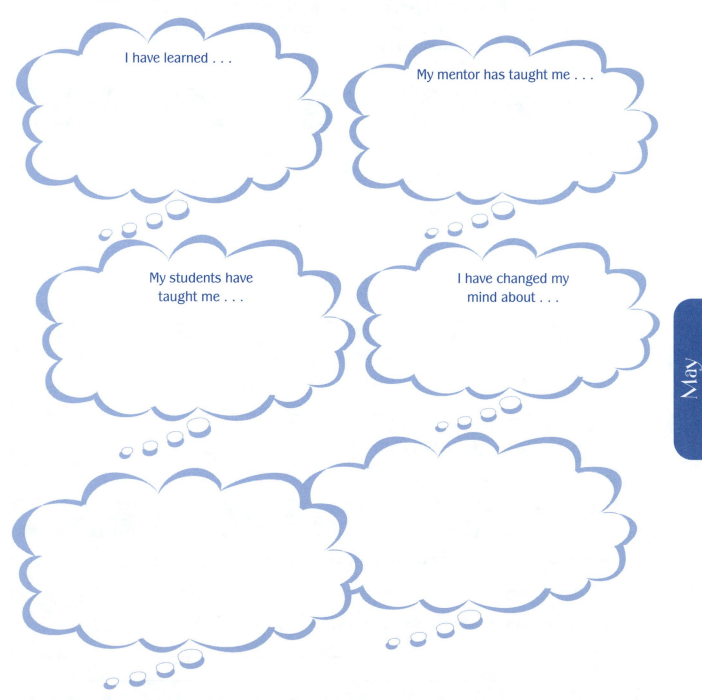

I have learned . . .

My mentor has taught me . . .

My students have taught me . . .

I have changed my mind about . . .

May

## ● SET GOALS Based on Your Needs for Next Month's Reflection and Discussion

**Directions:**

1. Review the pages in this chapter to determine what you need to revisit next month. Use these pages for possible goal ideas. Revisit any of these topics in your new-teacher support group or with your mentor.

2. Use the following to reflect on your anticipated needs. How can your mentor or other new teachers help you?

| Two New-Teacher Needs I Have Right Now! |
|---|
| 1. _____ <br> _____ <br> _____ <br><br> 2. _____ <br> _____ <br> _____ |

| My Mentor Can Assist Me in Meeting These Needs |
|---|
| My mentor can assist me in meeting need 1 by . . . _____ <br> _____ <br><br> My mentor can assist me in meeting need 2 by . . . _____ <br> _____ |

| My New-Teacher Support Group Can Assist Me |
|---|
| My support group can assist me in meeting need 1 by . . . _____ <br> _____ <br><br> My support group can assist me in meeting need 2 by . . . _____ <br> _____ |

# June

*A good teacher adds some humor
to teaching.* —Seventh-Grade Student

# Completing
# the Year
## Paperwork, Relationships,
## and Closing a Room

## New-Teacher Phase: Celebrate, Culminate, and Reflect

*"I felt like I was racing to get everything done
for the last day, and the next day everyone was gone!
No students, no directives from the central office, just me
feeling exhausted and exhilarated. I did it! I finished!
Now I know what I will do differently next year!"*

## INTASC Principles

Review INTASC Principle 9. Reflect on your own growth by rereading all your
journal entries in this book.

● **Principle 9  Professional Growth/Reflection**
The teacher is a reflective practitioner who continually evaluates the effects
of his or her choices and actions on others (students, parents, and other
professionals in the learning community) and who actively seeks out
opportunities to grow professionally.

## Completing the Year
### Paperwork, Relationships, and Closing a Room

This is the time to celebrate, culminate the year, and reflect on what happened. It has been a whirlwind for you! It is not over yet, because the cleanup and closing down take lots of time and energy, too. Stay upbeat as you move through the last month. Use your sense of humor and take time to remember the humorous things that have happened all year.

This chapter focuses on nuts-and-bolts work and the more serious side of looking at what actually happened this year. Continue to meet with the new teachers this month because you can support each other as you wind down the school year. Just like the orientation in August, the ending of the year brings up so many little details. Where do these books get stored? Who gets the report cards? How do I lock up and clean up my room? Your mentor has done this so many times it is second nature. It is new for you, so *ask* for help. Perhaps you need to create a closing-the-year survival kit!

Make time for meetings even though the schedules seem packed with other duties. This is the time to reap the ideas that you have been thinking about all year. This is when the harvest of work is complete. Videotaping or photographing your classroom to document what your first classroom looked like is important. Don't take everything down until you have recorded how you have organized your space. This is a reminder for next year! You will forget, so use this book to record your ideas.

Write a letter to your mentor and compliment your new-teacher support group. Create a ritual for ending the year. Review your journal entries beginning with that August day. See how far you have come in your thinking and learning. What did you enjoy? What was difficult for you? How can you use the information in this book for next year?

Acknowledge yourself for doing this work and go out with other new teachers to celebrate your accomplishments in becoming a teacher and surviving the first year. Bravo!

## ● Journal Entry

**Directions:** Read the cover page and the narrative for this month. How does this month's topic, the quotes, phase, and narrative overview relate to you right now? Are you comfortable with this topic? Do you need some help? How are you feeling right now?

Use your journal to record your thoughts, feelings, and questions in a free-flowing narrative. This page is for your personal reflection; it does not need to be shared as a written document. You are, however, encouraged to share excerpts with other new teachers or with your mentor as needed.

## Reflections:

*Today . . .*

Date _____

## ● PLAN Being Mentored . . . In Action!
### *Questions for Participating in a Quality Conversation*

Participating in a mentoring conversation requires you to be fully engaged. It requires listening and being open to what your mentor is sharing. This means you need to think about the questions you have and how to ask them. It does not mean you have to copy exactly what your mentor recommends, but it does mean you will reflect on the conversations and think about what makes sense for you.

Other new teachers have had these questions in June. Check the questions that you would like to discuss with your mentor or other new teachers in your school or district.

### New Teachers' Possible Questions:

_____ I need help in closing up my room. What should I do first?

_____ How should I reflect on my year? Will you meet with me?

_____ Should I seek feedback from others (students, parents, colleagues, etc.) to gain insights into my year?

_____ Do you have any final words of advice as I complete my first year?

_____ Other questions I have . . .

## ● Be Prepared
### *Your Mentor May Also Ask You Questions!*

### Mentor's Possible Questions:

_____ What did you learn about yourself as a teacher this year?

_____ What did you learn about your students and their families this year?

_____ How can I help you complete the year and do your June closing work?

_____ What can I do to assist you right now that would reduce your anxiety?

## ● Monthly Organizer
### *What I Need to Do Each Month*

**Completing the Year:**
**Paperwork, Relationships, and Closing a Room**

June

## ● PLAN Your Time Wisely

### *Reflecting on the Year: When Will You Do This?*

Your first year is over! Can you believe it? You know you didn't have enough time to do it all. You scheduled meetings when you could. Now it is important to carve out some time to close out the school year successfully and plan for next year! Don't skip this important step. It will help you plan for a successful second year!

- Meetings with your mentor that focus on closing out the year with paper-work, etc.
- Meetings with other new teachers so you can share what you are all doing to end the school year on a positive note with students
- Self-reflection to assess your year and make adjustments for what you will do next year. Read your journal entries and see how far you have come in your thinking and skills. This final summary self-reflection is important as you continue to develop as a teacher.
- Planning time to re-read all your journal entries
- Putting a portfolio together

# June Calendar

| MONDAY | TUESDAY | WEDNESDAY | THURSDAY | FRIDAY |
|---|---|---|---|---|
|  |  |  |  |  |
|  |  |  |  |  |
|  |  |  |  |  |
|  |  |  |  |  |
|  |  |  |  |  |

June

Key: B = Before school  D = During the day (preparation time or lunchtime)  A = After school

## ● CONNECT with People, Readings, Professional Associations, Resources, and Technology

▶ *What are the resources that exist in your school and community that could assist in closing out the school year?*

**Directions:**

1. Review your journal entry and questions from the *PLAN Being Mentored . . . In Action!* page for this month.

2. How can you *connect* with people in your school or district, readings, professional associations, resources, or technology to help you? You may complete this page by yourself, with your mentor, or with a group of new teachers.

### CONNECT *with People . . .*

Who in the school building (experienced teachers, other beginning teachers, custodians, secretaries, etc.) may be able to help with June needs?

Who in the community can assist in ending the school year?

How can parents be helpful in reflecting on your first year?

**Names:**

### CONNECT *with Readings, Professional Associations, and Resources . . .*

What have you read or used that would assist in ending a school year? You may refer to student teaching courses and readings. Your mentors will have protocols and materials that relate to this topic.

**Titles:**

### CONNECT *with Technology . . .*

Find websites and links that will provide information about

- The last week of school
- Reflection and writing about practice
- Beginning the second year
- Professional development opportunities

**Websites:**

## ● ACTIVITIES: Select Topics for Reflection and Discussion

### *What Should I Be Thinking about in June?*

This list of activities requires you to ACT either by reflecting on a topic or by discussing the topic with your mentor, other experienced teachers, or other new teachers. These activities are designed to stimulate your thinking. You do not have to complete all of them! Write in this book so you will have documentation of your thoughts and ideas for next year's planning.

### Completing the Year:
### Paperwork, Relationships, and Closing a Room

| FIRST STEP: Start the month with a new-teacher support group meeting! | | |
|---|---|---|
| ✓ | **Check the ACTivities from the following list that are most meaningful for you to discuss.** | **Page** |
| | ACT 1    Closing Procedures and Paperwork | 256 |
| | ACT 2    Videotaping | 257 |
| | ACT 3    A Letter to Myself | 258 |
| | ACT 4    A Letter to Future First-Year Teachers | 259 |
| | ACT 5    A Letter to Students and Parents | 260 |
| | ACT 6    A Letter to Your Mentor | 261 |
| | ACT 7    Classroom and Behavior Management Issues | 262 |
| | ACT 8    Looking at Student Work | 263 |
| | ACT 9    Communicating with Parents | 264 |
| | ACT 10   Preparing a Professional Portfolio: Table of Contents | 265 |
| | ACT 11   Sharing Your Professional Portfolio | 266 |

June

## ● FIRST STEP:  Host a New-Teacher Support Group Meeting

*Have snacks and water or soft drinks available. Hold the meeting in one of your classrooms so you can see teacher ideas in action. Rotate the classroom so you all have a chance to show and tell what you are doing. The host teacher could lead the meeting. Put a colorful sign on your door that says "New-Teacher Meeting. Please do not disturb." You may also want to invite other experienced teachers in the building or district who are also interested in sharing ideas. Set ground rules so everyone has a chance to talk. Use this monthly topic as a guide to keep you focused. Assign a timekeeper and set the next meeting date!*

**First:**  Welcome and introduce everyone. Take some time to go around the room and quickly share your name and grade level and one thing that is going really well!

**Then:**  Review your May new-teacher REFLECTion bubbles from this guide. If you haven't completed the bubbles, do it now, then discuss what you wrote and how you can help each other.

**Next:**  Review the SET GOALS page that you completed after the May support group meeting. How will you meet these goals?

**Begin:**  Discuss one or more topics from the ACTivities pages for this month. Which topic do most of you need to discuss right now?

**Network:**  Complete the CONNECTion page together.

**Acknowledge:**  Recognize what you have done so far this year and, instead of focusing on what you don't know, acknowledge your successes! Remind the group to complete the REFLECTion and SET GOALS pages on their own. The last day of the month is a good time to reflect.

**Share:**  End the session with compliments for each other and at least one practical idea for June. Take time to complete the Notes page.

## *Notes*

Something I learned in the group today . . .

Something I will use in my classroom from this meeting . . .

Questions I have to . . .

    Ask my mentor . . .

    Ask other new teachers . . .

    Ask administrators . . .

Idea to share at the next meeting . . .

June

# Closing Procedures and Paperwork

Ask your mentor how you should close your classroom and what must be handed in to the office the last day of school. Very often teacher induction programs do a great job orienting you to the beginning of the school year but forget to tell you how to end it. There are cultural norms in schools for doing certain things certain ways. This doesn't mean you shouldn't question things and try to improve upon them, it just means you need to ask your mentor what the procedures are for closing out the year.

### Possible paperwork

- Grades for students by certain dates
- Promotion cards or paperwork for retaining students
- Report cards for principal review a week before students get them
- Special needs student reports and IEPs
- Other

### Closing the room may involve

- Covering all the shelves with paper
- Removing all the books
- Putting things in storage
- Washing and cleaning furniture
- Other

You might be able to use students to assist you in some of these closing procedures. Often what happens at the end of the year is you don't know what is expected and you are left doing chores that other teachers have done in advance. Ask your mentor to help you get organized so you won't be spending days at the end of the year doing chores that could have been done earlier.

# Videotaping

It is not too late to videotape yourself teaching a lesson. In fact, this may be the perfect time! The end of the year is when you may have more confidence with the curriculum and experience in managing the classroom. You may also just want to videotape your classroom setup and bulletin boards, with your voiceover explaining why you set things up this way and what you want to remember for next year.

Suggestions for videotaping include the following:

1. You can focus the camera on the students, not you teaching. This way you can see the impact of your teaching on the students rather than your actual *teaching performance.* This may put you more at ease because you don't have to watch yourself on camera! It also allows you to see your students in action. Make sure all proper permissions slips for videotaping are completed before you begin.

2. Ask yourself what you would like to see on the tape, such as the way you open the class, your directions, and so on. Select two or three issues to investigate.

3. Observe the videotape with your mentor if possible. Discuss what is going on. Stop the tape at certain places and ask yourself what you notice or why you think a student is performing a certain way. Look at the two or three issues you listed earlier.

4. Ask your mentor if there is anything else she noticed in the tape.

### Using Videotape to Create a Class Documentary

Let the students get involved and create an end-of-the-year message for you!

### Using Videotape to Record the Room Arrangement and Bulletin Boards

Scan the room to record how things are set up, projects that are on the boards, and students' work. Think of other ways you could use videotape to remember what you did in year 1.

June

## A Letter to Myself

Write a letter to yourself at the end of the year. Share it with your mentor. Here is an example:

Date: _____

Dear Self:

This has been a year full of surprises and challenges. Some of them have been . . .


I have learned . . .


I feel good about . . .


Personally I appreciate the way I was able to . . .


I see myself . . . next year.


I really enjoyed . . .


I am confident that . . .


The best thing about being a first-year teacher was . . .


I am looking forward to next year because . . .


Sincerely,

# A Letter to Future First-Year Teachers

Prepare an open letter to next year's first-year teachers. Type the letter so that your letter can be copied and shared or placed in a binder for prospective new teachers to read. New teachers listen to other new teachers. This letter is a way of leaving a legacy to future teachers. If you are willing to talk to prospective student teachers, leave your email or phone number so you can be contacted.

Date _____

Dear New Teacher,

I have just completed my first year, and I have some advice for you as you begin preparing yourself for your first class.

_____

_____

_____

_____

_____

_____

_____

_____

_____

_____

_____

I have also attached two of my favorite lesson plans and an article that I found to be helpful.

Sincerely,


Grade Level

June

## A Letter to Students and Parents

At the beginning of the year you wrote letters to the parents. See September, ACT 10. Some of you may also have written letters to the students, too! Write a closing letter at the end of the year.

### Letter to Students

This open letter could thank the students for their cooperation. High school students would value this type of communication. It could acknowledge them for the work they did during the school year or highlight special activities. It does not have to be long, but it does have to be specific and authentic. Discuss ways you could include specifics without having to state every student's name. How could you use humor? How could this be personalized? Perhaps one sentence could be written at the bottom of each letter to that student? How is this different from the comments on the report card? Discuss other ideas for student letters with your mentor and list them here:

### Letter to the Parents

This open letter could refer to the original letter written in the fall. For most new teachers this will seem like a long time ago. Brainstorm what parents would want to hear in a letter. Would they care to hear information that is not about their own child? How could this letter be used to forward your standing in the community? Why is this a good idea? What are the downsides to doing a letter like this? If you are using a website, the letter could be posted there. Discuss other ideas for parent letters with your mentor and list them here:

# A Letter to Your Mentor

This is an opportunity for you to give feedback to your mentor. Ask him what he would like to know and then respond to that list. It might include the way he gave feedback, the number of meetings, and so forth. It takes courage for a mentor to ask for feedback. Possible topics to include in the letter are:

- Your mentor's strengths
- What you wish the mentor would do differently (This may be a delicate area to discuss. Perhaps it could be phrased as ways to mentor future teachers, or what you wish could have been done.)
- How the mentor helped you

Date _____

Dear Mentor:

I appreciated . . .

_____

_____

_____

_____

_____

_____

_____

_____

_____

_____

_____

Sincerely,

New Teacher

June

## Classroom and Behavior Management Issues

The year is coming to a close. One last month—and it could be the most difficult. You don't know what to expect and students are anxious to get out of school. Review all the classroom and behavior management pages in this book with your mentor and use them all!

Which ones really worked for you this year?

Which ones did not work and why?

Discuss with your mentor how you will close the year with your students. Ask for her ideas.

What will you do differently next year?

From Pelletier, Carol Marra. *Strategies For Successful Student Teaching: A Comprehensive Guide*, 2/e. Published by Allyn and Bacon, Boston, MA. Copyright © 2004 by Pearson Education. Reprinted by permission of the publisher.

# Looking at Student Work

### Review Four Major Components of Differentiating Instruction

As the school year comes to a close, it is important for you to stay on course and continue to modify and differentiate instruction. Don't give up! You may have tried different approaches during the year and have attended workshops, but you just can't seem to keep up with all the differing needs. Even experienced teachers find it difficult to find the time to analyze, sort, determine what the student needs next, determine what they need to do, and give a student a compliment. Stay connected to your support group and mentor so that you can keep trying this new skill of differentiating.

### Reflect on Your Year and Prepare for Year 2!

*How did you tap into students' prior knowledge?*

Did you pretest or interview students in a variety of ways to find out what they already know? Did you sort students into categories to assess the class' knowledge base?

*How did you teach content knowledge?*

Did you use varied reading levels for the same content? Did you use movies, interactive CDs, and other interesting materials? Did you reduce the number of vocabulary words or add enrichment words to provide the learners above or below standard with the appropriate amount of words to review?

*How did you use instructional methods?*

Did you continue to vary the way in which you delivered content? Did grouping, products and process assignments, graphic organizers, and varied strategies keep students engaged and responding to various learning needs?

*How did you use varied assessments?*

Did you use a varied number and kind of tools to assess student progress? Quizzes and tests are only one way. Knowing what students can do and being able to communicate that to them can make the difference in them staying in school. Are your students staying in school?

June

# Communicating with Parents

### A Year-Ending Report to Parents

The end of the year is a hectic and incredibly exhausting time for any teacher. You are especially overwhelmed because you have never done this before. You may have to hold a student back or give a report card that is less than satisfactory. Parents may or may not have been as cooperative as you may have liked and as a new teacher you many need some assistance from your mentor in sorting this out in a productive way. Despite all this, it is a time to celebrate the completion of a year and acknowledge what has been done successfully.

The final report cards will focus on the academic work, which is very important. However, there is an opportunity for you also to write a final note to parents that relates to the community of learners that developed in the classroom this year. Just as in the beginning of the year when you wrote a letter of introduction, it is important at the end of the year to write some kind of closing note to parents and students. This is your first year of teaching and it is important to take the time to reflect on what went well and to share that with parents and students.

Brainstorm ways you could possibly do this. A website with photos from the year? An email to all students and parents thanking them for a great year? A final newsletter?

List other ideas here:

Discuss why it is important to end the year with this parent communication even though the student is moving on to another grade. Find samples other teachers have done in the past. When should this final communication be sent? Celebrate and acknowledge what you have done!

# Preparing a Professional Portfolio: Table of Contents

_____ *Philosophy statement* (one page)

_____ *Professional profile* (third person, one paragraph)

Highlight your professionalism, additional activities, and strengths by including a professional profile in the portfolio. Like a biography, this narrative will provide your readers with highlights of your best features: languages you speak, places you have traveled, sports you play or coach, and skills you bring to teaching. Review your student teaching profile and resumé for ideas. Use an author's description on a book jacket to guide you.

_____ *Instructional practice*

This will be the major portion of your portfolio. It should be organized by competencies and/or themes with reflections and descriptions.

_____ Artifacts (photos, lesson plans, etc.)

_____ Diagrams

_____ Audio and video with written explanation of what is on the tape

_____ Samples of student work

_____ *Appreciation notes, public appreciation* (from parents, teachers, students)

If you saved notes people wrote to you that were positive, include them on a page titled *Appreciation*. If they relate to a lesson, you may include them on that page.

_____ *Evaluation reports* (from supervisor and cooperating teacher)

_____ *Guest register* (last page)

This page is for people to sign and date when they read your portfolio. Space for one brief comment should be included.

### Optional

Create your own teaching trifold brochure that highlights your skills, goals, and attributes. Design it like a business brochure to be shared with parents.

From Pelletier, Carol Marra. *Strategies For Successful Student Teaching: A Comprehensive Guide*, 2/e. Published by Allyn and Bacon, Boston, MA. Copyright © 2004 by Pearson Education. Reprinted by permission of the publisher.

June

## Sharing Your Professional Portfolio

Organize a portfolio-sharing party with all the mentors and new teachers in your district. Plan a social event that brings everyone together to celebrate what you have learned. Design a "Guest Register" page that will allow readers to sign your portfolio and make a brief comment about it. Have food and music, and place the portfolios on a table where guests can flip though them and sign the guest register. If time allows, videotape each new teacher with their portfolio. Let them show one page and have them share one thing they learned by completing this portfolio.

Share your portfolio with

- The principal or department chair
- The school committee
- Faculty at the school
- Parents at an open house in the fall
- Students the first day of school of the second year
- New students who come in later in the year
- Community business partners

Think of other ways you can share your professional work!

## ● REFLECTions

**Directions:** Reread all the reflections you completed from August through May. Then complete all the bubble prompts here. Share your responses with your mentor.

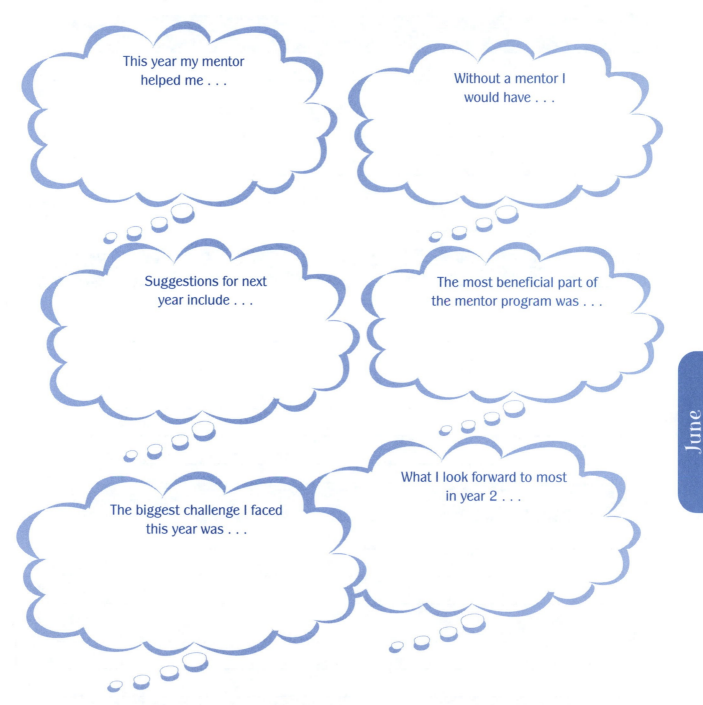

This year my mentor helped me . . .

Without a mentor I would have . . .

Suggestions for next year include . . .

The most beneficial part of the mentor program was . . .

What I look forward to most in year 2 . . .

The biggest challenge I faced this year was . . .

June

## ● SET GOALS for Year 2!

**Directions:**

1. Review the SET GOALS pages you completed this year.
2. Based on your own needs, what would you set as goals for yourself for next year?

| Summary of My Two Most Important Needs This Year |
|---|
| 1. _____ |
| _____ |
| _____ |
| 2. _____ |
| _____ |
| _____ |

| Goals I Have for Next Year |
|---|
| 1. _____ |
| _____ |
| _____ |
| 2. _____ |
| _____ |
| _____ |

| My New-Teacher Support Group or My Mentor Can Assist Me to . . . |
|---|
| 1. _____ |
| _____ |
| _____ |
| 2. _____ |
| _____ |
| _____ |

# ● Reflecting on Your First Year of Teaching

Your first year is over! Can you believe it? You know you didn't have enough time to do it all. You met with your mentor and your new-teacher support group as often as you could. Now it is important to carve out some important time to close out the year successfully and plan for next year! Make sure you

- Find out about paperwork that needs to be completed at the end of the year
- Create a closing activity with your students to celebrate their progress
- Reflect on the year using the Final Journal Entry on the next page
- Complete your portfolio and submit it for approval (if required)

What else needs to be done?

June

## ● Final Journal Entry: Reflection for Year 1

Reread all your monthly journals written in this book and write a *final impression* that captures your first year of teaching. Notice what you were writing about all year. What did you write about in certain months? Were there common themes to your writings? What did you notice about your development as a teacher from August to June?

Date _____